© 2016 Clover Stornetta Farms, Inc.

Published by Clover Stornetta Farms
PO Box 750369
Petaluma, CA 94975

All rights reserved. No part of this book may be reproduced in any form without written permission from the publishers, except by reviewers who wish to quote brief passages.

The names and marks:
Clo the Cow, Clover Stornetta, Clover Petaluma, Clover Stornetta Farms, and Clover Organic Farms are the property of Clover Stornetta Farms, Inc., a California Corporation, and are used with permission.

ISBN: 978-0-692-76236-3

Book Design: Anne Vernon

Printed in 2016

Printed in China through Global Interprint, Inc.
800 Warrington Road
Santa Rosa, California 95404

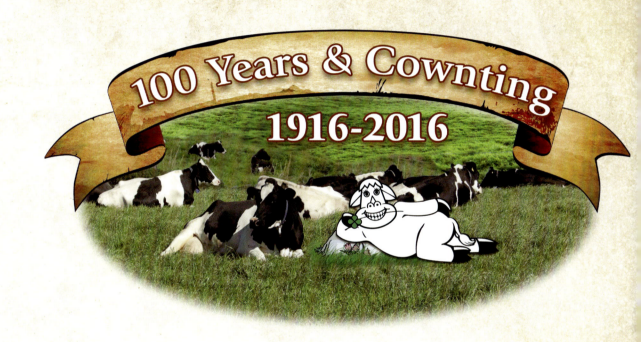

I have worked with Clover and Clo the Cow for 21 years.

I met Gene and Dan Benedetti within a week of each other, and was introduced to both by master adman, Jim Benefield. I found both father and son charming, sincere, and brimming with vitality, curiosity, and personality.

I was lucky to get to know all three men: Gene and Dan Benedetti, and Jim Benefield. Sadly, Gene and Jim are no longer with us, but both were LegenDairy, unique, charismatic individuals that I am so glad to have known.

I worked closely with Dan Benedetti for many years, and found him to be a marvelous visionary for his wonderful company, Clover Stornetta Farms. Now his son, Marcus Benedetti, commands and steers the direction of this rare and great company as it enters into its second century, and continues Clover's proud tradition of care for its customers, its family farms, and its pure and ethical products.

Thank you Clover for all your work and integrity in thought, word and deed. And thank you for letting me help envision Clo for you. Clo never ceases to grip my imagination, and causes me to chuckle as I draw her.

What a wonderful way to spend my day!

Anne Vernon

LegenDairy Clover

By Anne Vernon
Contributing Writers:
Karen Pavone, Tim Tesconi, & Gaye LeBaron
Editor: Karen Pavone

Contributing Billboard Artists:
Anne Vernon, Gordon Cockroft,
Art Zadina, Craig Curtiss, Susan Evason,
Bill Knight, Lynn Morgan, Bill Nellor,
David Oshiro, Jim Wakeman, & Adrienne Reid

Contributing Billboard Punsters:
Jim Benefield, Anne Vernon,
Margo Gallamore, the Clover Crew,
and the much appreciated Public

"My Grandfather did something that was very rare and very, very difficult. He not only created and launched a business, but he maintained his ideals and adhered to his convictions every step along the way until he retired.

He lived by the Golden Rule: 'Do unto others as you would do unto yourself,' and he evaluated every business decision and relationship through the prism of that belief. That's what endeared him to so many people. There was nothing false about him.

Thinking back now, my grandfather's legacy was living by that rule, and consistently applying it in every situation he encountered. That's how I remember him, and I think that's how others remember him best. He was a leader. He was a coach. He was a mentor. And he was a civic icon that valued integrity above all else."

Marcus Benedetti, President Clover Stornetta Farms

LegenDairy Clover
A century of dairying to be great

Foreward by Gaye LeBaron

In Memory of Gene Benedetti by Tim Tesconi 8

Interviews with the Founding Family
Founding Father Dan Benedetti 12
President Marcus Benedetti 14
Clover Country Comics 16
Stories & Good Wishes from Clo's Knit Family 18

Dairying to be Great: the Story of Our Brand
A Visual Timeline of the Origin of a Legend 22
The Evolution of Clo, the Cow 24
What Clover Stands For 26
Family Farms 28

The Billboards
1969 to 2016 35

THE PRESS DEMOCRAT

GAYE LeBARON'S NOTEBOOK

Clo the Cheerful, Jacques the Mean

Short of calling upon all members of the Jacques Cousteau Society within earshot to write letters threatening to withdraw financial support, I can't think of how we can help Clo the Cow. But I weep for her.

These celebrated friends of the whale and the dolphin, with their $14 million organization, are suing our hometown cow for 1.2 million clams because, on a billboard south of Sonoma advertising Marine World, she was pictured in a diving mask, swimming with a shark. The legend read: "Jacques Cowsteau." Big wet deal!

Clo has many identities. She's been Christopher Cowlumbus, Vincent Van Clo, with only one ear; Wolfgang Amadeus Moozart; Bogart, complete with trench coat, on the "Here's Lickin' at You, Kid" board; the Moona Lisa. None of these people sued — and they're all more famous than Jacques Cousteau. As a matter of fact, the grumpy old mariner should be flattered to be included.

These Clo boards are educational — like the one being prepared now that features the world-famous cow as Claude Moonet beside his lily pond at Giverny. How many milk companies give you art history with their advertising?

Clo is cheerful. She shows up at parades and school carnivals, dishes free ice cream at the fairs, has provided free milk to almost as many kids as there are fish in Cousteau's sea. And Cousteau wants to put her out of business? Merci beaucoup, M'sieu Meanie!

Clo is to Sonoma County what that mouse is to Anaheim. Don't mess with her.

WEDNESDAY, NOVEMBER 17, 1993

The Daily Minimum

CLO'S ENCOUNTERS of the Curd Kind: I've long been a fan of Clo, the dewy-eyed punning cow featured on the Clover-Stornetta Dairy billboards in Marin, Sonoma and Napa counties. Currently, Clo wears a Wagnerian horned helmet (stop the moosic!) and warns "It Isn't Clover Till the Fat Lady Sings." Not one of her greats but wait: Some time ago, Clover-Stornetta hooked up with Marine World for a billboard showing Clo swimming with a shark and identifying our heroine as "Jacques Cowsteau." Pretty funny? Not to the humorless Jacques Cousteau Foundation in N.Y., which filed a cease-and-desister. Dan Benedetti, pres. of Clover-Stornetta, didn't argue. The billboards were changed but that didn't end the matter. Last wk., Benedetti was rocked when the Cousteau Foundation filed a $1.2 million suit in Fed'l Court here, charging the dairy with "copyright damage." Ain't it enough to curdle your milk? Next week, Clo appears on a new set of billboards showing her dressed as a World War I doughboy and sipping milk out of a wine glass over the caption, "Clover There." If there's a George M. Cohan Foundation, Benedetti will hear.

★ ★ ★

THE PRESS DEMOCRAT, TUESDAY, MAY 23, 1995

GAYE LeBARON'S NOTEBOOK

20 years of Clo's pun and games

When does an advertising gimmick step out of the realm of commerce and into the genre of folk art?

This and other questions will be answered next month when an exhibition of "Clo Art" opens in Santa Rosa.

It was inevitable that Clo, the ubiquitous hometown cow, would someday gather all of her billboards together in poster form for an important retrospective called, of course, "Clo's Look."

She's already dipped her dainty hoof into global politics through a Clo's encounter with Jacques Costeaux. Now she is, as her recent waterlilies billboard indicates, mooving in on Claude Moonet.

Monet may be packing them in at the DeYoung in San Francisco but just wait until Clo's show opens.

The 20 years' worth of prize-winning puns and progressively wacky art work courtesy of Clover-Stornetta Farms and Benefield, Levinger & Associates, will go on exhibit June 9 at the Cultural Arts Council's SoFo Gallery on South A Street in Santa Rosa and run well into July.

Foreward by Gaye LeBaron

It's hard to write anything about the history of Clover Stornetta Farms and where it stands on the path to the region's agricultural glory that doesn't begin with Clo the Cow.

Still, Clo, beloved for her comedic charm, is a relatively new character in a story that begins a century and a half ago. The trailblazer was a nameless (well, maybe Buttercup, or Bossy) family cow, tied to the back of a creaky wagon, grazing with the oxen at night, sustaining a family on its way to California -- where, it was said, the valley land grew grass tall enough to hide a horse.

The land, the climate and the proximity to the cities on San Francisco Bay all conspired with that pioneer cow to lure immigrants with Old World farming skills. In the 1850s a fleet of sturdy little "butter boats" carried dairy products to those cities and created a cluster of small creameries in the coastal communities.

By 1860, dairying had become the leading "money crop" in an area with a fast-growing agricultural reputation. And, by the early 20th century — when Sonoma County's varied farm production rated eighth in the entire nation, the dairy cow was still the queen of Sonoma County.

Meanwhile, those hometown creameries, in competition now with the Central Valley and other emerging "Ag" giants, found the need to cooperate. The Petaluma Co-operative Creamery, the base from which Clover Stornetta Farms would be launched, dates to 1916.

The story of the next 100 years is what you'll find in this book. Meanwhile, we also celebrate close (Clo's) to 50 years of our favorite cow, a point at which we must pause to consider the forces that created her.

Gene Benedetti had been manager of the Petaluma Co-op for 20 years when Lee Levinger, founder of the county's first ad agency, suggested a billboard with a cartoon cow. It was Gene's job to sell this idea to his board of directors, a panel of old-style dairymen, many of whom thought it was nonsense to advertise milk with a cartoon. "They wanted a real cow," Gene told an interviewer years later.

A lot of serious lobbying resulted in a very narrow (Clo's) victory with dairyman Jack Dei, chairman of the board, casting the deciding vote.

Artist Bill Nellor, a Levinger employee, drew the first Clo for a "Support Your Local Cow" billboard west of the freeway in Rohnert Park in 1969.

In 1972, Clo settled into the fertile mind of Levinger's successor, Jim Benefield, who also proved to be "outstanding in his field," winning multiple awards for his agency.

It was Benefield who kept the puns coming for a quarter-century, assuring us that — as certain as the cows coming home at milking time, there would always be new Clos just around the bend.

Still a product of VeVa Communications, successor to the Benefield-Levinger agency, Clo has established herself as — well, I guess you could say — the Mickey Mouse of the North Coast.

Clover employees in cow costume show up everywhere — in parades, celebrations, farmers' markets, handing around free ice cream cones at county fairs.

Her biography, titled **Wholly Cow**, was published in 2000. And she has been honored with an exhibit at the Sonoma County Museum.

So, read all about it, the whole Clover story. This volume is the bigger picture, a (Clo's) look at the success story of an enterprise that has faithfully followed that "real cow", tied behind the settlers' wagon, into North Coast history.

In Memory of Gene Benedetti

~ FOR HIS GREAT LOVE FOR HIS FAMILY, CLOVER, AND THE PEOPLE & DAIRIES OF NORTHERN CALIFORNIA

1919-2006

By Tim Tesconi, for The Press Democrat

Gene Benedetti, a Sonoma County farm boy who became a World War II hero and later a devoted family man, successful businessman and community leader, epitomized the nation builders known as "the greatest generation."

Benedetti, founder of Petaluma's Clover Stornetta Farms and patriarch of a family that long has been part of Sonoma County's social and political fabric, died January 13, 2006. He was 86. Shortly before his death, Benedetti attended Clover Stornetta's Christmas party, leading 400 people in a rousing round of "God Bless America," his favorite song.

"Dad had an insatiable love for this country, a love that really came to fruition after his experiences during World War II," said son Dan Benedetti of Petaluma, who followed his father as president and then board chairman of Clover Stornetta Farms, the Bay Area's largest independent dairy processing company.

As a Navy officer and skipper of the lead landing craft in the American invasion of Omaha Beach on D-Day in 1944, Benedetti survived what he would always remember as "the worst and longest day of my life." It was an experience that shaped his life, but one that he didn't talk much about until recent years.

Gene with the Silver Star Medal for his service in Normandy on D-Day

Newlyweds Evelyn and Gene Benedetti

After returning home, Benedetti channeled his energies into raising a family, earning a living and making Sonoma County a better place to live. Like many members of that generation, he looked to the future, not the past.

"After Normandy, I never think about yesterday and I never worry about tomorrow," Benedetti said in interviews marking milestones of the D-Day invasion.

Benedetti was an astute businessman who built a dairy products empire with the Clover Stornetta brand. Under Benedetti's stewardship, Clo, Clover's cartoon cow, became a community icon known for her corny puns and toothy, bovine grin.

For decades, advertising executive Jim Benefield of Santa Rosa handled the Clover account, working hard to corral both Clo and Benedetti.

"Gene left a huge void. He was a crusty old rascal and I'll miss him very much," Benefield said. "I worked with him for 23 years, and we would fight over every aspect of Clover's advertising, then go out and have a martini and laugh about it." Benefield said Benedetti had a Legendairy life that was well lived.

"Gene was unique, a Navy hero at Normandy, a dedicated family man, a loyal friend and a shrewd businessman," Benefield said. "In a fiercely competitive field, he not only kept Clover Stornetta in the battle, he made it thrive."

A gregarious guy, Benedetti worked crowds like a veteran politician, slapping backs and giving a handshake so firm it hurt. He called men "Buck" and women "Doll" and, because of his abiding spirit, no one was offended.

Benedetti was born Dec. 19, 1919, in a small farmhouse in Sonoma, the youngest of three children of Italian immigrants Giocondo and Pia Benedetti. The family later lived on a ranch in Santa Rosa before saving enough to buy their own farm, a 13-acre spread in Cotati. The Benedettis operated a dairy and raised livestock and poultry on the diversified farm where Gene Benedetti would develop his lifelong work ethic and deep understanding of agriculture.

Sons Herm & his wife Marilyn; Dan & his wife Anne with Gene & Evelyn

The small farm, which members of the Benedetti family jokingly called the Ponderosa of Sonoma County, later became Benedetti's home, an outpost where family and friends were always welcome. Benedetti and his wife, Evelyn, who died in 2004, were known for their hospitality.

"For me, visiting Gene and Evie's house was like ascending to Camelot," said godson Doug Pricer. "Evie was always beautiful and gracious. Gene was always welcoming and generous. There was always great food and warm fellowship. Anyone who walked through Gene's door, be it the president or the porter, were family. He loved us all."

Benedetti attended Cotati schools and went to Petaluma High School. A gifted athlete and a born competitor, he became a football star at Petaluma High, Santa

Rosa Junior College and the University of San Francisco. At USF, he participated in a history-making sporting event, playing center and linebacker against a Stanford team coached by Clark Shaugnessy that used the T-formation for the first time. Stanford beat USF that day, went 10-0 that year, and went on to win the Rose Bowl by beating Nebraska.

At war's end, Lt. Benedetti came home to a job as assistant football coach and history instructor at SRJC. George Dondero, then manager of Petaluma's Cooperative Creamery, was looking for young veterans who knew the area and could speak Italian because there were many Italian dairy farmers in the area and the cooperative wanted their milk. Dondero offered Benedetti a job as a milk buyer. To sweeten the deal, he played upon Benedetti's love of football, offering to help him establish a semipro team in Petaluma. Gene said yes to the offer to work at the creamery, but no to Dondero's overture to help finance a team. Gene and his good friend, Bob Acorne, felt their community involvement coupled with their teammates and leadership was enough to bring this new endeavor together.

The result was the Petaluma Leghorns, a Benedetti-coached powerhouse that dominated semipro football in the Bay Area for 10 pre-TV years between 1948 and 1958. Benedetti's Leghorns, playing to crowds as large as 5,000 at Petaluma's Durst Field, became a Bay Area football legend. In 1948, they scored 398 points in 12 games, third-highest in the nation behind only the San Francisco 49ers and the University of Nevada.

As TV and pro sports caught America's fancy, the Leghorns faded and finally folded in 1958. But Benedetti found his star rising in the North Bay milk industry. He succeeded Dondero as co-op manager in 1955. With six partners, he bought the co-op's Clover dairy brand, which dates back to 1913, acquired Stornetta Dairy in Schellville and established Clover Stornetta Farms in 1977.

Clover has become an outstanding dairy products company leading the nation in redefining sustainable, high quality dairy farming. Clover continues to pioneer an agricultural movement that makes a difference in the way we drink milk and the way a milk company is looked upon.

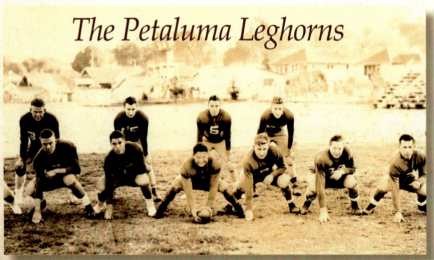

The Petaluma Leghorns

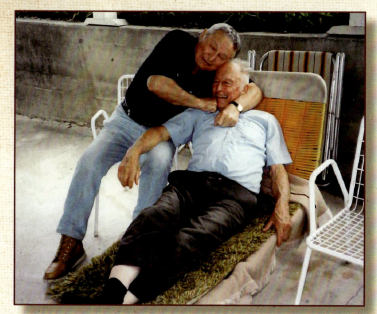

Gene with Al Stornetta

A cameo moment with Father and Son, Gene & Dan Benedetti

Dan Benedetti

Dan Benedetti and his father, Gene Benedetti, were two of the original founders of Clover Stornetta. Dan succeeded his father as President of Clover in 1986, and followed his father's philosophy of community service.

When Gene Benedetti decided it was time to hand off Clover business operations to his son Dan in 1986, Dan knew he had big shoes to fill. "Pops was a very bold, courageous individual in life as well as business," he reflects thoughtfully, "and I don't think Clover could have been started by anyone else."

Dan, along with his father Gene, Paul Ross, John Markusen, Bill Van Dam, and Gary Imm made up the six original owners that purchased Clover following the 1977 fire that devastated the original processing plant at Petaluma Cooperative Creamery. "My father's choice of business partners was purposeful and not without instinct and insight," Dan reflects. "Dad had worked closely with all of them, and knew they had what it takes."

His father also believed the group had the fortitude to stand together and face the challenges that confronted them in getting the new company off the ground. That determination served them well.

The partners had no collateral to start the business, and the banks wouldn't extend a loan because the venture was considered too high risk. Dan credits his father's ability to build relationships as the glue that would bring all the pieces together. It was Gene's personal connections with the Hansen family, who owned Crystal Creamery, along with Al and Charlie Stornetta, who owned Stornetta Dairy, and his longstanding ties to Petaluma Co-Operative Creamery that led to those companies putting up the capital to finance the new "Clover Stornetta Farms".

With their goal in reach, the owners put everything on the line to make the deal work. "It was a very tense time, but we believed in what we were doing. The rest is history," remembers Dan.

With Dan as president and Gary Imm as CEO, Clover opened a fully automated state-of-the-art Petaluma-based processing facility in 1991, which enabled production to increase three fold. With this new technology in place, the company continued to grow while remaining ever committed to the core ideals and principles established by its founding father.

Dan didn't know it yet, but Clover's business was about to be tested.

Monsanto and rBST

In 1994 representatives from Monsanto came knocking at Clover's door touting a newly developed "wonder drug" called rBST. It was a synthetic growth hormone designed to artificially stimulate milk production in dairy cows. Monsanto was not the only company vying for business at the time. Big Pharma companies including Eli Lilly, Upjohn, and American Cyinmaid all had patents pending for similar drugs.

During the meeting, Monsanto representatives did their best to persuade Dan that the newly developed hormone would "increase profits and revolutionize the dairy industry, but appear seamless to the consumer."

Dan recalls asking them one question: "If this product is **that** good, and you've spent millions to produce it for the market, then why are you here talking to me? How much money have you spent telling consumers how great this product is?"

It was a pivotal moment in Clover's history.

Though other dairy companies were rushing to jump on board, Dan turned Monsanto down flat. "The more we raised concerns about rBST, the more apparent it was there were a lot of questions that weren't being answered," he remembers.

"Before that meeting I questioned if we were on the right path as a company," Dan recalls, "but after that meeting, the answer was abundantly clear to me. I thanked them (Monsanto) for coming, but I went on record as opposing rBST that day. I knew without a doubt that our customers would not want this, and we could not compromise their trust or the health of our dairy cows."

Monsanto representatives responded with stunned silence, then left the office.

"My decision was based on keeping our relationship with our consumers intact," says Dan. And with that commitment, Clover became the first dairy west of the Mississippi to offer milk certified free of the growth hormone rBST.

Setting the Bar Higher

That same year, Clover developed the **North Coast Excellence Certified (NCEC)** program; a trail blazing set of rigorous guidelines that holds its family owned dairy partners to the highest standards for animal welfare, sustainability, and environmental stewardship.

"We wanted to stake our claim as having the best milk in the industry," says Dan, "and that meant focusing on the qualities that sets Clover apart from other dairy companies. No one else out there has a certification program like ours."

NCEC stipulates that Clover cows are never treated with the growth hormone rBST, never cloned, and are cared for under the American Humane Certified animal welfare program. In fact, Clover was the first dairy in the United States to be **American Human Certified** by the American Humane Association.

In addition, NCEC requires Clover dairies to demonstrate best environmental practices of their land and resources by having systems in place to improve soil condition, protect water quality, and preserve wildlife habitat. In return for compliance, Clover has rewarded its dairymen with economic incentives — an unprecedented policy that demonstrates the company's loyalty to its partnering family farms.

By working with its producers to uphold these quality standards, Clover has insured that its milk is the benchmark of the dairy industry. To quote Pete Hardin, Publisher of The Milkweed, "Clover is quite possibly the cleanest milk in the United States."

Always working to stay ahead of the curve, Clover was also early to recognize the importance of offering an organic product choice to Clover customers. Today, Clover's fluid Organic dairy products carry the Non-GMO Project Verified Seal which further demonstrates the company's ongoing dedication to putting the consumer first.

Serving the Cowmunity

From the beginning, Clover embraced the importance of community outreach and service to its hometown of Petaluma and Sonoma County. Dan had witnessed the power of that example first hand through his dad Gene.

"My father was a giant, and he made an impact in the community that people still remember today," he says. "Pops felt strongly that our business should have a close connection with the community."

"He believed, 'You take care of home, and you take care of the people close to you,'" Dan continued. "That's just the way it was and how it was going to be. There was no question about it. I was proud to carry on the tradition of philanthropy he started at Clover."

For two decades, Dan continued to lead and carry on his father's legacy at Clover before passing the baton to his own son, Marcus, in 2006. Reflecting thoughtfully on his career, he sums up his tenure in the family business in a single sentence: *"When you love what you do it ceases to be work, and becomes a labor of love."*

Marcus Benedetti

IF YOU CAN TALK WITH CROWDS AND KEEP YOUR VIRTUE, OR WALK WITH KINGS - NOR LOSE THE COMMON TOUCH..."

Rudyard Kipling, **If:** *A Father's Advice to His Son*

Marcus Benedetti, current Chairman of the Board, CEO, and President of Clover Stornetta, also grandson to Founder Gene Benedetti, and son to Founder Dan Benedetti

As the current President and CEO of Clover Stornetta, Marcus Benedetti brings his own unique vision to the company. Since taking the reins from his father, Dan, in 2006 he has worked tirelessly to continue the trail blazing tradition of excellence established by his predecessors.

Marcus is proud to represent the third generation of his family to carry Clover's legacy forward. Since stepping into the spotlight a decade ago, his tenure has been a balancing act between embracing the company's future, and paying homage to its distinguished past. Like his father and grandfather before him, Marcus has faced challenges that have tested his leadership ability and defined his place in the company's history. He feels the gravity of the legacy entrusted to his care and is determined to set a course that would make his father and grandfather proud.

"My grandfather was an incredible man," he reflects with reverence. "His passion for life was forged out of his early childhood experience as the son of Italian immigrants, and later as a distinguished veteran of World War II. These experiences gave him grit, tenacity, and a strong work ethic which made him a successful businessman and community leader. He was a role model I always looked up to."

Marcus credits his father, Dan Benedetti, as an early pioneer in the movement toward sustainability long before his peers in the dairy industry were talking about it.

"I remember when Monsanto visited my dad in 1994 to tout the virtues of a new growth hormone called rBST," says Marcus. "He saw immediately that Big Pharma was looking to profit at the expense of what was best for the consumer, and sent them packing."

"Not long after that meeting, Dad began laying the groundwork that led to Clover's

North Coast Excellence Certified (NCEC) program, which established stringent guidelines for stewardship and humane husbandry practice that has been the backbone of our company's philosophy ever since. My father also spearheaded the movement to transition into organics. It was a very exciting time in Clover's story," Marcus recalls.

It was that excitement and momentum that inevitably drew Marcus to the family business. After his business studies from the University of Alaska, Fairbanks, Marcus was still living in Alaska when he felt the call to return to his hometown Petaluma.

"What Dad was doing intrigued me," he recalls. "I had fond memories of he and my grandfather talking about the business around the fireplace at our home. I wanted to have a relationship with my Dad like he had with his father."

But coming home was no guarantee of a career at Clover. Though the business is family owned, every family member who wants to work for the company must be vetted to see if they are capable.

Like those who came before him, Marcus knew he would need to prove himself and earn his place. As a teenager, and during summers home from college, he had already cut his teeth learning different aspects of the business. He started working in the cooler and spent night shifts in receiving, then advanced to the truck shop where he became a delivery driver bringing milk to restaurants and schools along his route. He even suited up as Clo the Cow and hoofed it through parade routes around Northern California.

Learning the business from the ground up gave him key insights into how the company worked at all levels and how Clover dairy products actually flowed into the community. Eventually, Marcus worked his way into sales and earned his own territory in the Bay Area and Southern California.

When his father Dan retired in 2006, he proudly turned Clover operations over to Marcus with his full approval and support. Their mutual respect for each other and close, affectionate relationship remains intact to this day.

Since taking his place at the helm of Clover, Marcus has successfully put his unique stamp on the company by expanding both Clover's product line and its reach to new markets beyond its Northern California roots. He also continues to look to the future by seeking new and innovative ways to grow the company sustainably including incorporating green technology at all levels of production.

"We are striving to reconnect the American dairy farmer to the consumer in a positive way," says Marcus. "We're telling a different story by being transparent and showing people where their milk comes from. Our biggest challenge and opportunity is bringing our message and values to a new audience."

That personal connection to its customers is what has set Clover apart through the years. "My dad was a master at cultivating genuine connections with people," Marcus reflects. "He always had his ear to the ground and not only welcomed feedback, but took it to heart in his decision making. It was that direct relationship with our customers that fundamentally changed Clover's business. And once we built that trust, we made sure we delivered on our promise. That's what we've always strived to do."

Marcus hopes the legacy he has inherited will not end with his generation. "I look at myself as a temporary steward of something I can pass on to my children," he once told a reporter at The Press Democrat (July 2014). No doubt when the time comes, those that follow will take their turn at being vetted to earn a place in Clo's Quarters.

Four generations:

*From Left:
Marcus Benedetti
holding son Jack,
Gene Benedetti,
Dan Benedetti*

Clover Country Comics!

∼Charming, Retro, Sweet, Heartfelt...the Softsell Message from the Adorable Character known as Clo the Cow.

Hand-drawn Clo — you think she's simple, but she's not. Clo is a plump, jovial Holstein with enormous character and ethics. Sometimes she doesn't get her own puns, but she always loves a good joke. She is as transparent as a gossamer firefly wing in a lovable bovine body. Her toothy grin never fails to put a smile on our face.

Her babies — Cookie, Lucky, and Poppy, arrived in 2002 with "Dairy Tails," which helped Clo tell the story of her beloved Clover. Bullie Boy, Clo's admirer, came on the scene in 2004 when their "Quartship" blossomed.

These pages show nine of the forty Clover Country Comic strips, drawn between 1969 and 1972, in which Clo made her debut appearance in Sonoma County. She got her charm and silliness from her creator, Lee Levinger, and his art director Bill Nellor. Levinger and his partner, Jim Benefield, owned a Santa Rosa-based ad agency, and Benefield was responsible for launching Clo's clever one-line billboard puns. Those memorable billboards created a public phenomenon that cemented Clo as Clover's iconic moo-lebrity.

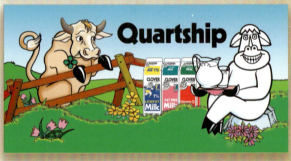

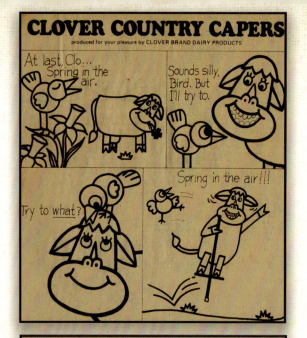

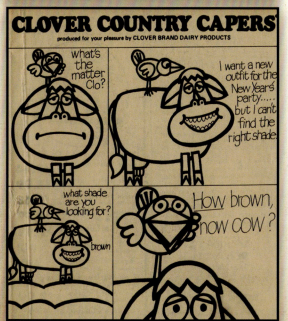

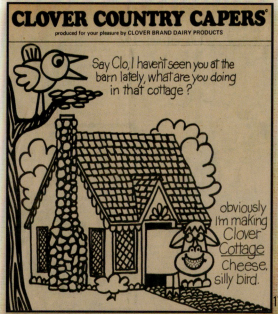

Stories & Good Wishes from Clo's Knit Family

It has been a great Partnership between our two "Local" companies.
Clover Stornetta has evolved with today's consumer needs while maintaining their high involvement towards our "Communities".

We are proud to be on the same "Team" and wish you another 100 years of "Clo" Success.
Dick Gong,
G&G Supermarket

Clorrespondence

Clo

bright eyed

light-headed, light-hearted

clenching a perfect clover

between grinning milky whites

she dons virgin maiden semblance

and conjures

seven waxen cardboard dwarfs

tiptoeing through tulips

choreographed

across galactic Copernican milky ways

in supreme courteous, jestered design.

Essentially,

outstanding in her field,

she is but one bueno moo of a kind!

© Pierre Chevalier

Since we first opened our doors at Oliver's in 1988, our relationship with Clover and the Benedetti family has remained among the most important vendor partnerships that we have enjoyed. We have had the great pleasure of working with three generations of the Benedetti family, starting with Gene, and then Dan, and now Marcus, through the years, and have watched the Clover brand grow and thrive as they have made it stronger and stronger. Our company cultures also align well: the people at Clover share our commitment to quality and community, and we both celebrate good humor, too.

Congratulations to the Benedetti Family and everyone at Clover on a century in business.

Tom Scott, CEO, Oliver's Market

Congratulations to Clover Stornetta Dairy on 100 years of business! Gene M. Benedetti, founder, passed away in 2006, but his legacy lives on in the second and third generation of family members and employees who focus on maintaining not only top quality, but on doing things greener. Over 68 years ago Vallergas began working with Clover Stornetta, and has always found this company to have the highest of standards. My warmest wishes for many more years of serving the community.

Ray Sercu,
President, Vallergas Market

The Best Dairy in California with the highest quality!
The Best Service in California and with outstanding communication.
The Best Company in California and yes, Clover has been exceptional for many years.
Bill Daniels,
United Markets, Owner/President

Congratulations to Gene, Dan and Marcus and the whole Clover family for an unbelievable accomplishment! You have all made an incredible difference in the milk industry by providing consumers with the best quality milk available. Congratulations and best wishes for the next hundred years!

Mike Stone, CEO
Mollie Stone's Markets

Clorrespondence

Dear Clover Stornetta,

My name is Remy Labesque. I'm 13 years old and live in Glen Ellen. We drink "Clo's" milk every night at dinner. But when I was looking at the milk bottle while eating, I noticed something about Clo. Now either I'm crazy or I'm totally psychic but when I look at Clo on the milk carton I see 4 other animals besides Clo!

The first two I saw were the parrots on Clo's head (they are shown from profile.)

The next thing I saw was the frog; (Clo's nose and mouth):

And finally the last thing I saw could have been two versions of the same illusion; I see either two birds in a nest poking their heads out for food, or I see a bird flying seen from the top.

Thank you very much.

Sincerely,
Rémy Labesque

Clo...what's the latest scoop?
Clover Country Ice Cream... delicious!

For over 20 years, New Leaf Community Markets has partnered with Clover Stornetta Farms to bring our customers the highest quality dairy products available. One has to understand that New Leaf, a grocer committed to the highest standards in the natural and organic sector, is particularly picky about the brands that it supports, and that it considers Clover to be a key brand partner is to be truly valued. That Clover has always been about sustainability, about small family farms, about not feeding unhealthy growth hormones to the cows so they produce more milk, and about producing the best-tasting products in their category are all good reasons why we have valued this relationship. Not to mention that the family and the people behind this product operate the company with a level of integrity that is rarely found.

Scott Roseman, Founder, New Leaf Community Markets
Congratulations on 100 years.

Joanie Benedetti, Granddaughter of Gene Benedetti

Soon after starting at Clover, I worked on creating a marketing video for the company to talk about what we represent and who we are, which sounded like great fun. I've never been a video producer, so I thought, "Let's jump into this and give it a try."

We were filming a segment that has Clo the cow in it and we were taking a bunch of still photos as well. We wanted to get Clo the cow in a field with a bunch of real cows. So Karen Hall, who was in charge of Clo and community relations at the time, said, " No problem, I'll get in the Clo costume."

So we go to Jim Riebli's dairy in Petaluma. He says, "Go out in this front field and the cows, you know, they're curious. Once you're out there they should come around you and be in the background, so that should make for some great photos."

We get into this field and have the videographer and the photographer set up. And getting into the Clo costume is pretty cumbersome, so I'm there, helping Karen get in the costume. And once you're in that costume, you can't see very well, you have a fan going so you can't hear anything very well, and so we're getting her in and I zip her up and I look up. And all these cows are coming towards us. And one is coming a little bit faster than the rest and I'm just thinking, "Uh oh, it's a bull, it's a bull!"

I remember ducking, trying to look at every angle to see if it was in fact a bull. I couldn't see any horns. I yelled, "Karen, run, run!" Trying to direct her to get out of the field, she can't hear anything, she can't see anything, and then all of a sudden this cow pops up right in front of her face. She must have turned shades of white, I can only imagine, inside that costume.

But it was just a very curious heifer!!!

Clo, Caen, & Cousteau

As a celebrity in her own right, Clo made a few high profile friends through the years.

Pulitzer prize-winning columnist and San Francisco icon Herb Caen was one of them. Caen was known nationally for penning his daily column in the San Francisco Chronicle which ran for nearly sixty years. He wrote with his finger on the pulse of the Bay Area, and his way with words had a profound influence on pop culture slang. It was Herb who first coined the term beatnik, and popularized the word hippie during San Francisco's infamous Summer of Love in 1967.

Turns out he also developed a "cow crush" on our holstein mascot Clo, and that cow-nection would come in handy down the road.

As the story goes, on a whim Dan Benedetti asked Jim Benefield to send a billboard drawing of Clo to Herb Caen. To Dan's delight, Caen made mention of it in his column. "He said there was this company up in Sonoma County that had a funny-looking cow named Clo and everybody loved her," remembers Dan. "I called him up to thank him and said, 'You don't know what the power of the pen means to a small company like Clover. Maybe I'll send you a billboard from time to time.'"

"Sure, send them down," Caen agreed. And so began the relationship between Clo and Caen. As it turned out, it pays to have friends with pull in the press.

This is where Jacques Cousteau enters the story.

"It all started over a billboard we had at Sears Point in partnership with Marine World," says Dan. "It showed Clo in underwater garb next to a treasure chest filled with Clover products and the pun, 'Jacques Cowsteau'."

Apparently, Cousteau's people failed to see the humor and filed suit against Clover.

"Jeff Goodby, a friend of mine who worked on the California Milk Processors Advisory Board and the "Got Milk" campaign, called me after he heard about the lawsuit." said Dan. "He told me, 'Hold on to your hat. I've had experience with Cousteau's legal team and they will **NEVER** let this go.'"

When the ensuing ruckus got back to Caen, he reached for the phone and called Dan to get Clover's side of the story. Then he did what Herb Caen did best. He wrote a commentary in the Chronicle and brought the issue to the attention of a bigger audience. "He just trounced the Cousteau Society," Dan recalls.

The piece went viral. It circulated throughout the United States, and was broadcast live throughout Canada on CBC. From there it went to Australia, then Germany, and finally reached Cousteau's home turf: France. People were furious! Within a week the controversy was over.

Caen's commentary solved the legal cownundrum and created a positive publicity storm that brought Clover attention on a domestic and international stage.

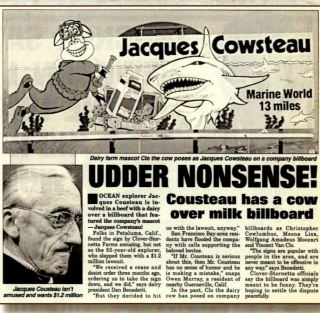

The Press Democrat

Nov. 20, 1993

Clover Historical Timeline

1916

Petaluma Cooperative Creamery began distributing Clover Brand dairy products to stores and residential customers in the Petaluma, CA area. As Petaluma and the rest of Sonoma and Marin Counties continued to grow, so did the Co-op. Clover Brand products began showing up in nearly every store and household in the North Bay.

1929

Petaluma Cooperative Creamery started to bottle **milk** under the **Clover Name**. The first day's bottling was fifty quarts.

1933

Cottage Cheese was added to the Clover line of dairy products with a production rate of 150 pounds per day.

1968/69

Clo the Cow first appeared as the official mascot for Clover Brand products, with a rapid revision in 1969. Clo has graced billboards in Northern California ever since with her magnificent smile and witty puns.

The first Clo in 1968

Clo got a facelift in 1969

1975

Tragedy strikes on the twenty-second of August at 1:42 am when the Petaluma Cooperative Creamery is destroyed by the largest fire in Petaluma's history. The disastrous blaze claimed the bottling & processing plant and cooler.

1977

Clover Stornetta Farms was born from the ashes of that devastating fire. Following a decision by the Co-op not to rebuild the facility, the original partners of Clover purchased the wholesale distribution business from Cal Co-op and Stornetta's Dairy in Sonoma, California in August of 1977.

1986

Gene Benedetti, President & Chairman of the Board, asks his son **Dan to succeed him as president.**

1991

Clover Stornetta opened a **new state-of-the-art milk processing facility** in Petaluma which replaced the Stornetta Dairy in Sonoma as its processing plant. The new fully automated facility enabled Clover to triple the output of the old plant with virtually the same manpower.

1994

Clover turned down Monsanto's newly developed synthetic growth hormone, **rBST**, and launched the **North Coast Excellence Certified (NCEC)** program which set the most rigorous quality standards in the industry for Clover's family owned dairy partner producers.

1999

Dan Benedetti pioneered the way for Clover as an early entrant into **organics** which naturally fit Clover's philosophy for sustainability.

2000

In September 2000, Clover Stornetta Farms became the first dairy in the U.S. to be certified by the American Humane Association (AHA) for their animal welfare program, **American Humane Certified.**

2006

Dan transitioned out of his role as Clover's President and became Chairman of the Board. His son, **Marcus Benedetti,** became the third generation leader at the helm of Clover.

Press Democrat Sunday, Aug. 30, 2015

2015

Dan Benedetti retires and Marcus assumes his role as **Chairman of the Board,** while maintaining his responsibilities as President & CEO of Clover.

2016

Clover turns 100 Years Old!

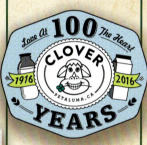

The Evolution of Clo, the Cow

1969: First Billboard

Like all of us, Clo's appearance has changed and matured through the years. It's hard to fathom in light of her ultimate success, but at the outset her image was a Clo-se call. Early iterations of the toothy bovine had some people scratching their heads. At first, even Clover's founder, Gene Benedetti, wasn't sure about Lee Levinger's depiction of his mascot.

"Hell, she doesn't even look like a cow!" Dan Benedetti remembers his father commenting on the artist rendering. "Look at those big teeth on the top and bottom. I don't think the Board of Directors will accept this mascot for the company."

Lee Levinger, Clo's creator, offered to deliver a pitch to the Board but Gene wouldn't hear of it.

"I will talk to them and reason with them," he said, "but if they don't accept it, they don't."

It was far from an easy sell. Many of Clover's producers expressed doubt. They said, "It doesn't work. It doesn't look good! And so on," Dan remembers. But Gene had a feeling about Clo, and despite the opposition he went with his gut.

"Let's do one billboard for six months and see what kind of reaction we get from the public," Gene offered as a compromise. "If there's a positive reaction, we will have the answer to our question."

And that's what they did. The rest is history.

1989: Tip Clo through your two lips

What Clover Stands For

Clover Stornetta Farms is exceedingly proud to be recognized as a leader in the dairy industry on a local and national scale. Our relentless pursuit of excellence and commitment to quality are the hallmarks of our business. Instead of following the herd, we have chosen to blaze a trail that sets us apart from our peers.

To start with, we listen to our loyal consumer base. We not only welcome their feedback, but use it to guide us in how we produce our dairy products. Keeping open lines of communication with our customers and staying in touch with their expectations is fundamental to our business every day.

Based in Petaluma, California we are born and grazed in the heart of Sonoma County, and proud to be Made Local!

Head and Hooves Above the Rest

Do you know what sets Clover apart from our competitors?

Clover was the first dairy west of the Mississippi to offer milk free of the hormone rBST. When other dairy companies decided to embrace Big Pharma in their operations, Clover took a step back and evaluated what was right for our producers, our cows, and our consumers. As a result, one hundred percent of Clover milk comes from cows not treated with rBST.

Second, Clover's family owned dairy farms are an invaluable legacy that embody the best in environmental stewardship and humane husbandry. Many of our partner producers come from multi-generational dairying families and we are proud to help them preserve this time honored way of life.

Third, Clover is committed to sustainable agriculture. We have developed stringent guidelines for the care of our dairy cows and best practices for responsible land stewardship.

Finally, Clover cares by giving back and supporting local organizations. Each year Clover gives back up to 10% of its pre-tax profits through donations and sponsorships supporting the causes that matter to us and the communities we touch.

CLO STANDS FOR
QUALITY ★ FAMILY ★ INTEGRITY

AMERICAN HUMANE ASSOCIATION

At Clover, we love our dairy cows and place the highest value on their health and wellbeing. Our partner family farms in Sonoma and Marin Counties follow strict standards for the humane treatment of the animals in their care. Together, we produce the highest quality milk pool in the country.

The cows on our producer farms lead a good, stress-free life. They have access to open pasture with plenty of walking area, a diet of fresh grass, hay and grains, and clean bedding when they go to sleep. In addition, Clover cows are raised without antibiotics and hormones such as rBST. These criteria are evaluated on site by an independent inspector and approved by a third party before our family farms achieve the certifications required by Clover.

In September 2000, Clover Stornetta Farms became the first and only dairy in the U.S. to be certified by the **American Humane Association (AHA)** for their animal welfare program, American Humane Certified.

This annual certification by the AHA means that you can enjoy Clover products knowing our dairy cows are:

Free to live and grow in a humane environment under conditions and care that limit stress.

Free to enjoy a healthy life, benefiting from injury and disease prevention and rapid diagnoses and treatment.

Free to readily access fresh water and a diet that maintains full health and vigor.

Free to express normal behaviors and live in an appropriate and comfortable environment that includes sufficient space, proper facilities, shelter, a resting area, and the company of their own kind.

Check out www.thehumanetouch.org to learn more about the American Humane Association and how you can support the American Humane Certified program.

OUTSTANDING IN OUR FIELD

In 1994 Clover Stornetta Farms became the first dairy processor to elevate milk from a commodity to a specialty food by establishing the **North Coast Excellence Certified (NCEC)** program.

NCEC holds our family owned dairy partners to the highest standards for animal welfare, sustainability, and environmental stewardship in our industry. These stringent guidelines surpass the requirements set by both state and government agencies making them the most rigorous in the dairy industry.

NCEC requires our dairymen to demon-

strate best environmental practices of their land and resources by having systems in place to improve soil condition, protect water quality, and preserve wildlife habitat. In return, Clover rewards their excellence with economic incentives.

By working with our producers to uphold these quality standards we have insured that Clover's milk is the benchmark of our industry. To quote Pete Hardin, Publisher of The Milkweed, *"Clover Milk is quite possibly the cleanest milk in the United States."*

We have earned that reputation by vigilantly monitoring and checking the bacteria counts of our milk every day which is well beyond the once-a-month industry requirement. Because of this, Clover milk stays fresher, tastes better, and has a longer shelf life than other brands.

In 1994, we took the unprecedented step of having an independent auditor verify our NCEC milk quality standards. The certified public accounting firm, Pisenti & Brinker, completed an examination of our NCEC program policies and procedures.

"In our experience, most companies don't go to these lengths to verify their product claims."

*Carmel Brown
Accounting & Auditing Manager
Pisenti & Brinker*

Our Family Farms ~ Clover's Trust

Aggio Dairy
Location: Santa Rosa, CA
Generation: 5th
With Clover since: 2013

Amos Brothers Dairy
Location: Santa Rosa, CA
Generation: 3rd
With Clover since: 1999

Bivalve Dairy®
Location: Point Reyes, CA
Generation: 6th
With Clover since: 2006
Organic Since: 2006

Bucher Farms
Location: Healdsburg, CA
Generation: 2nd
With Clover since: 1999
Organic Since: 2008

Buttke Dairy
Location: Sebastopol, CA
Generation: 6th
With Clover since: 2013

Circle LC Corp
Location: Petaluma, CA
Generation: 3rd
With Clover since: 2012

Dolcini Jersey Dairy
Location: Nicasio, CA
Generation: 6th
With Clover since: 2011
Organic Since: 2011

Doug & Cathy Ielmorini Dairy
Location: Nicasio, CA
Generation: 6th
With Clover since: 2011
Organic Since: 2011

George Grossi & Son Dairy
Location: Novato, CA
Generation: 4th
With Clover since: 2012

Gerald Spaletta Dairy
Location: Petaluma, CA
Generation: 5th
With Clover since: 2011
Organic Since: 2015

Henry & Steve Perucchi Dairy
Location: Bodega, CA
Generation: 2nd
With Clover since: 1999
Organic Since: 2013

Ielmorini Moody Dairy
Location: Valley Ford, CA
Generation: 4th
With Clover since: 2012
Organic Since: 2013

Jim Riebli Dairy
Location: Petaluma, CA
Generation: 3rd
With Clover since: 1999
Organic Since: 2012

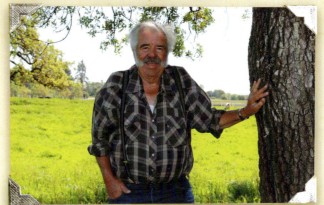

Joe Pinheiro Dairy
Location: Santa Rosa, CA
Generation: 1st
With Clover since: 2013
Organic Since: 2016

Johnson-Neles Dairy
Location: Sonoma, CA
Generation: 3rd
With Clover since: 2012

Kehoe Dairy
Location: Inverness, CA
Generation: 4th
With Clover since: 1999
Organic Since: 2006

Lafranchi Ranch
Location: Nicasio, CA
Generation: 5th
With Clover since: 1999
Organic Since: 2006

McClure Dairy
Location: Inverness, CA
Generation: 4th
With Clover since: 1999
Organic Since: 2007

Moretti Family Dairy
Location: Tomales, CA
Generation: 4th
With Clover since: 1999
Organic Since: 2012

Mulas Dairy Company
Location: Sonoma, CA
Generation: 3rd
With Clover since: 2012
Organic Since: 2008

Neil McIsaac & Son Dairy
Location: Tomales, CA
Generation: 5th
With Clover since: 1999
Organic Since: 2012

Renati Dairy
Location: Bloomfield, CA
Generation: 3rd
With Clover since: 2011
Organic Since: 2013

Robert Giacomini Dairy
Location: Point Reyes, CA
Generation: 3rd
With Clover since: 2006

Roy King Dairy
Location: Petaluma, CA
Generation: 3rd
With Clover since: 2014

Spaletta Ranch
Location: Petaluma, CA
Generation: 5th
With Clover since: 2011
Organic Since: 2013

Terrilinda Dairy
Location: Santa Rosa, CA
Generation: 4th
With Clover since: 2012

Vevoda Dairy
Location: Ferndale, CA
Generation: 2nd
With Clover since: 2015
Organic Since: 2006

The Benedetti Family
Three generations of Benedettis
Circa 1980s

1969-2016

A Retrospective

*47 Years of
Clo's Billboards*

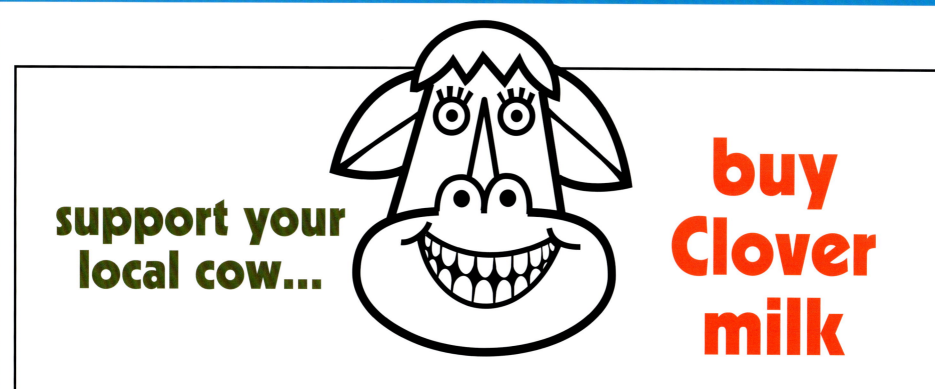

Cow jokes? I've herd them all!

1969

Clo-brainer:
How many times does a cow's heart beat per minute?

A: *60-70 beats per minute.*

1969

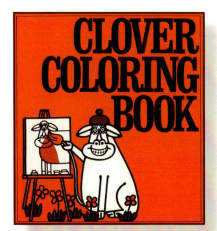

Circa early 1970's

1971

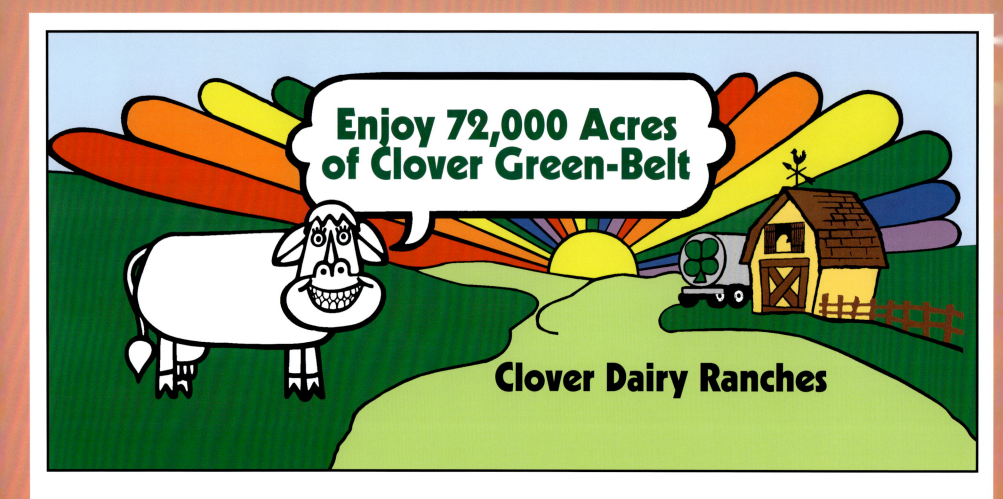

1974

Clo's line

Clo-brainer: *Our beloved founder, Gene Benedetti, came up with the idea of Clo the Cow to be Clover's mascot, but who was the first person to draw Clo?*

A: Bill Nellor

1976

1977

 # Clearly Ahead

Clo, the advertising genius
Graham Hovis, 6th grade

One of the reasons Clover-Stornetta milk is so popular may be partly because of advertising. The winners of the annual print media competition in the billboard category are the "Supreme Quart" billboard, "Slender in the Glass" billboard and "Half Galleon" billboard.

Some of Clover's other eye-catching billboards are: Behind Clo's doors, Mooing pitcher star, Clearly Ahead, Clo's line, Clo's uncounters of the curd kind, Clo's quarters, New designer Clo's.

Other favorites are Outstanding in her field, Moona Lisa, Wolfgang Amadeus Moozart, Christopher Cowlumbus in the Moo World, Miss Sonoma Cowntry, van Clo's favorite pitcher, Lip Clo through your two lips, Two Clo's fur comfort, Here's lickin' at you, and Cowabunga.

Next time you drink a glass of Clover-Stornetta milk, think about how much work went into that glass of milk.

The Press Democrat

1981

1982

Clover was the proud sponsor of the Johnny Cash Show, 1984

1984

Clo-brainer: *In what year were plastic milk jugs introduced in the U.S.?*

A: 1967

Q: What do you get when you cross an elephant with a dairy cow?

A: Peanut Butter.

1985

*Clover Butter Float
Circa 1929*

1986

*Don't cry over spilt milk.
Turn the udder cheek and mooove on.*

1986

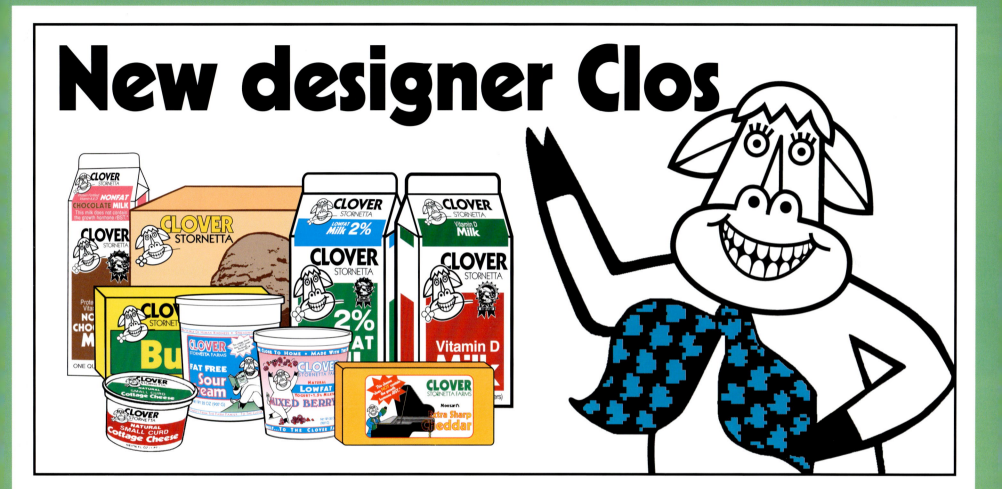

Clo-brainer:
What breed of cow produces the most milk?

A: Holstein

1987

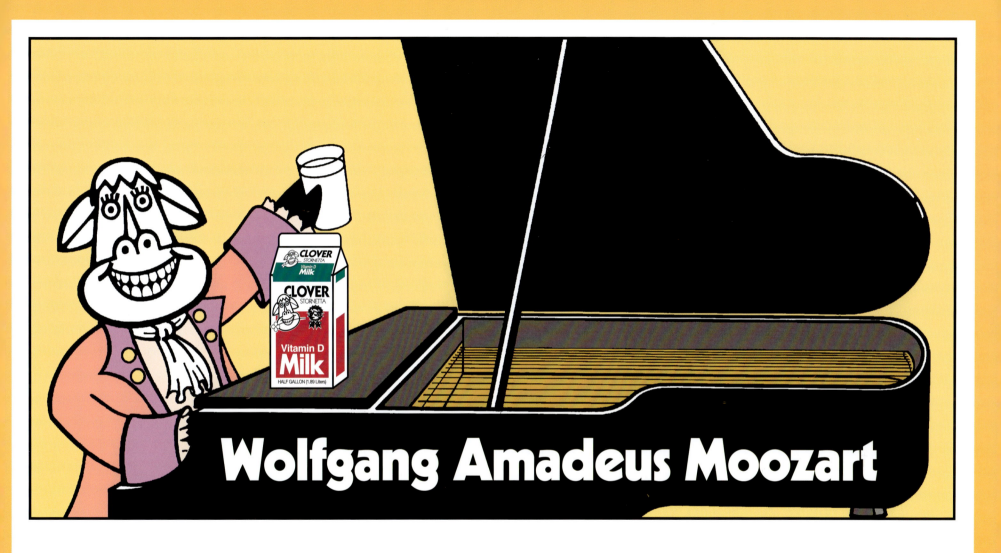

Clo-brainer:
How do you tell the age of a cow?

A: *Count the rings on its horns.*

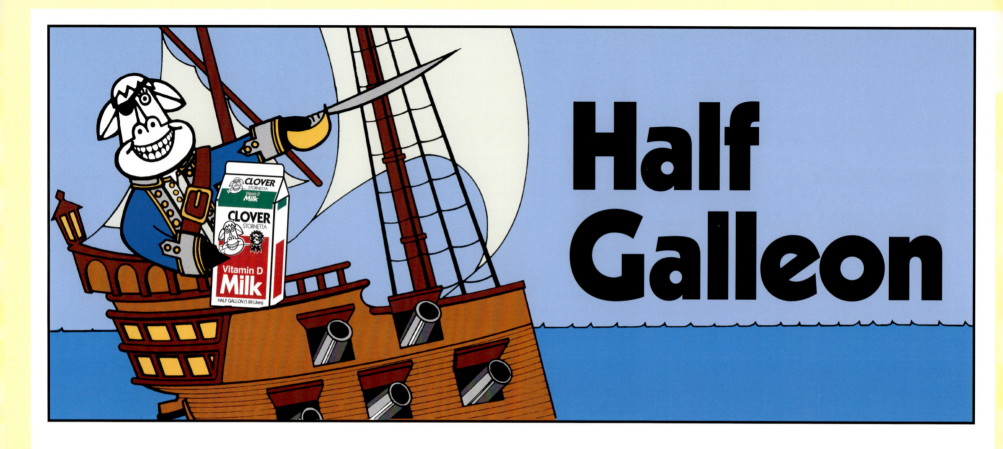

Clo-brainer:
Roughly how many squirts of milk from a cow's udder are in a whole gallon?

A: 350

1988

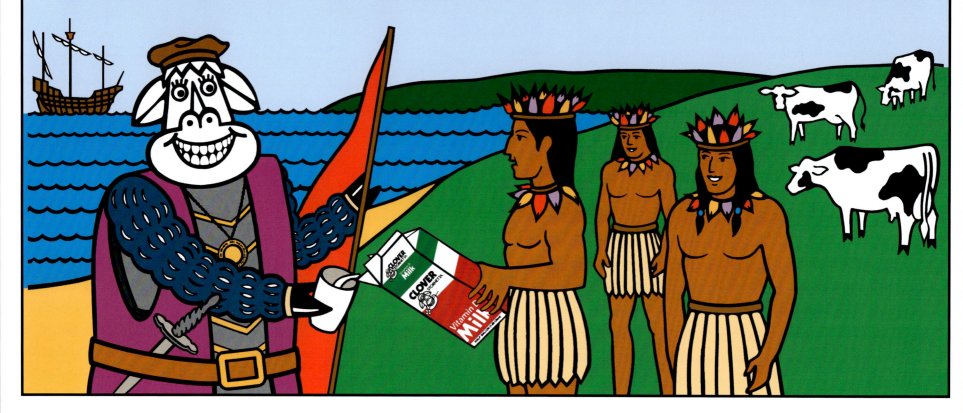

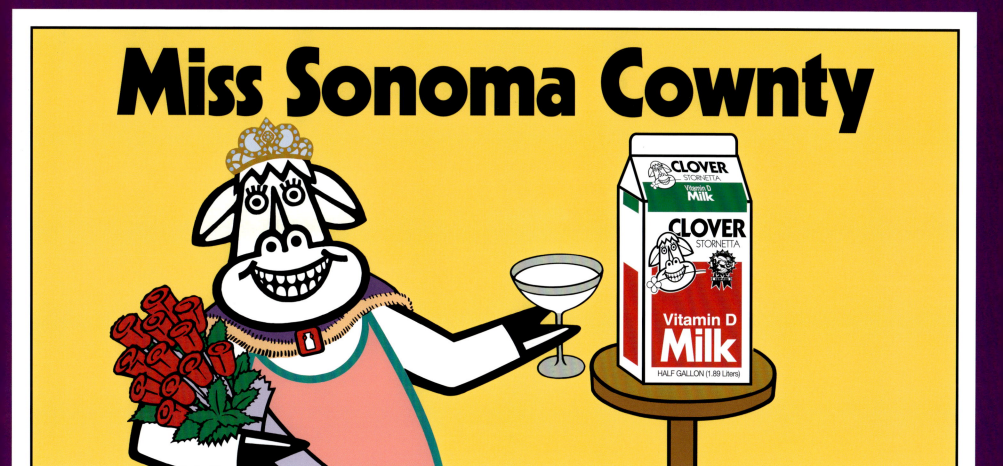

Clo-brainer:
How many pounds of saliva can a cow produce in one day?

A: *125 pounds*

1989

Dan Benedetti with Tiny Tim, inspiration for the 1989 "Tip Clo through your two lips."

1989

Q: *What do you call a cow who works for a gardener?*

A: *Lawn moo-er.*

1989

Clo-brainer:
How does a cow graze?

A: Cows don't bite grass. They actually curl their tongue around it.

1989

Who's the new heifer?
Never seen herbivore!

1990

Moona Lisa

A classic pitcher.

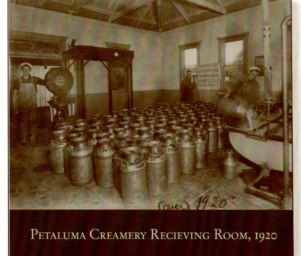
Petaluma Creamery Recieving Room, 1920

1990

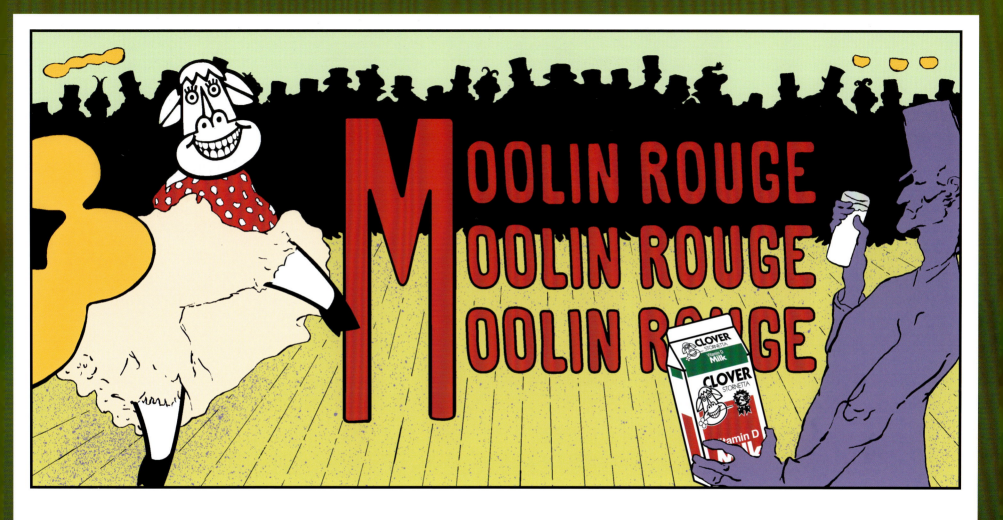

1991

Something in the way she moos,
attracts me like no udder lover.

1992

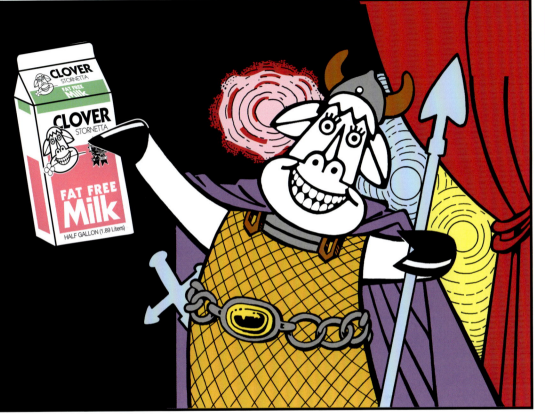

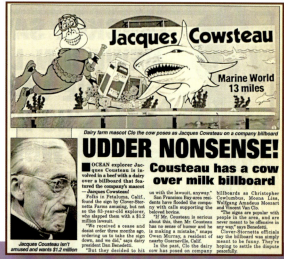

The Press Democrat

1993

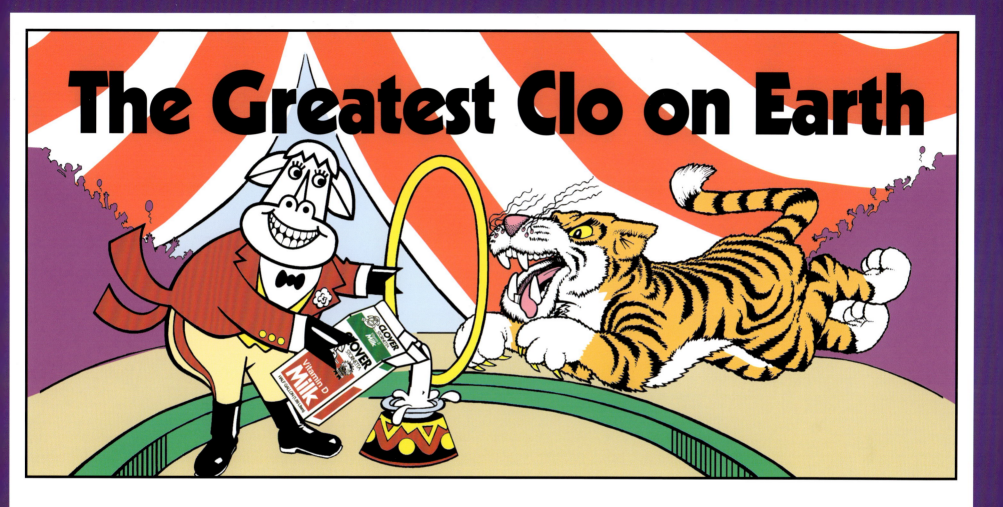

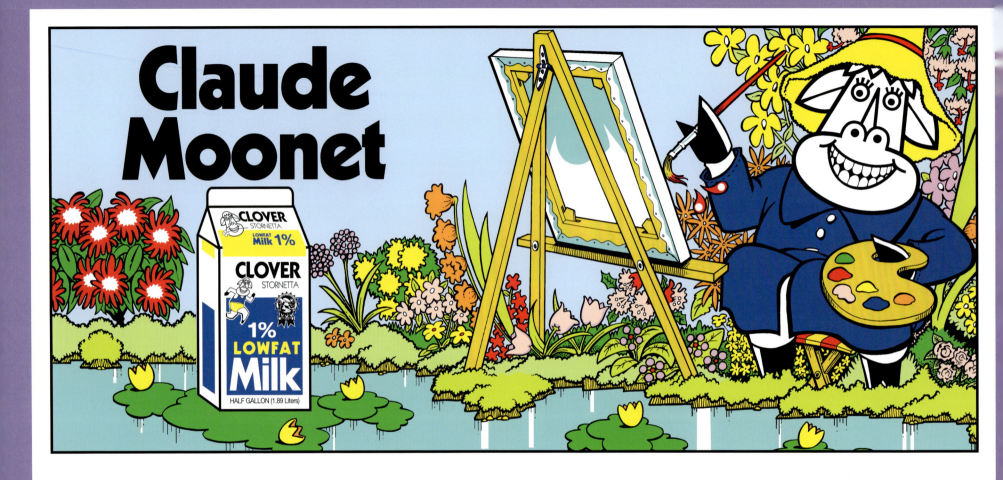

Q: What do you get when you cross a cow and a duck?

A: Milk and quackers.

1993

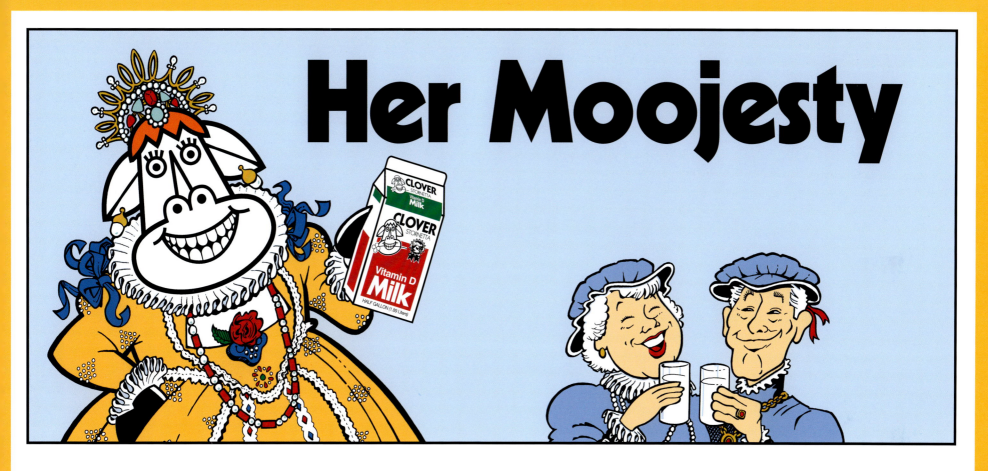

Her Moojesty

 *Cows display emotions and have been shown to produce more milk when they are treated better and as individuals.*

This is underlined by Clover's certifications with North Coast Excellence and American Humane Association.

1994

The oldest cow ever recorded was a Dremon Cow named 'Big Bertha' who died 3 months just before her 49th birthday on New Years Eve, 1993...

1994

...'Big Bertha' also holds the record for lifetime breeding as she produced 39 calves.

Clo-brainer:
How many times does a cow sit down and stand up each day?

A: *About 14 times each day.*

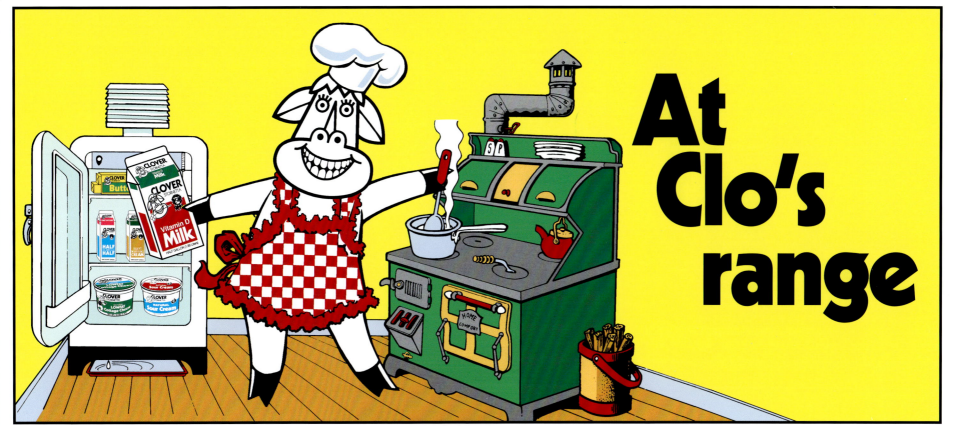

Stocking up on Clover products in this vintage 1960's photo.

Clo-brainer: *How many glasses of milk are produced by a cow over her lifetime?*

A: 350,000

1995

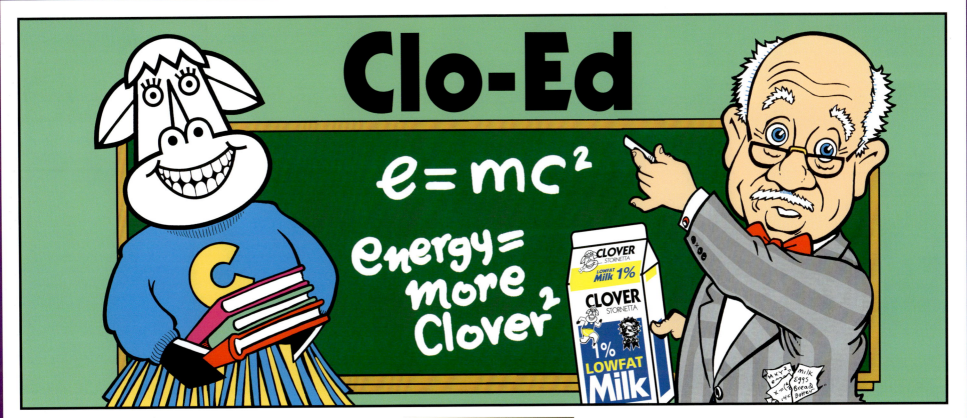

Clo-brainer:
How well can cows see?

A: *Cows have an almost 360° panoramic vision.*

Clo-brainer: *How many pounds of whole milk does it take to make one gallon of ice cream?*

A: 12

1995

Vintage Clover brand ad with the first 1968 Clo.

1996

1996

Just "Beat It",
Vintage Clover brand ad circa 1950's.
Michael Jackson was not born until 1958.

Q: What does a greek cow say?

A: Mu.

Q: What does a french cow say?

A: Moo la la.

1996

Q: *What happened to the lost cattle?*

A: *Nobody's herd!*

Clover Delivery Trucks

First Double Transport — 1960

1997

Mt. Rushmoooer

Clo-brainer:
How much water does a cow drink daily?

A: *About 25–50 gallons; that's almost a bathtub full.*

1997

Clover's earlier version of the Milk Way, circa 1950's

Riding the rails at our new processing plant.

1998

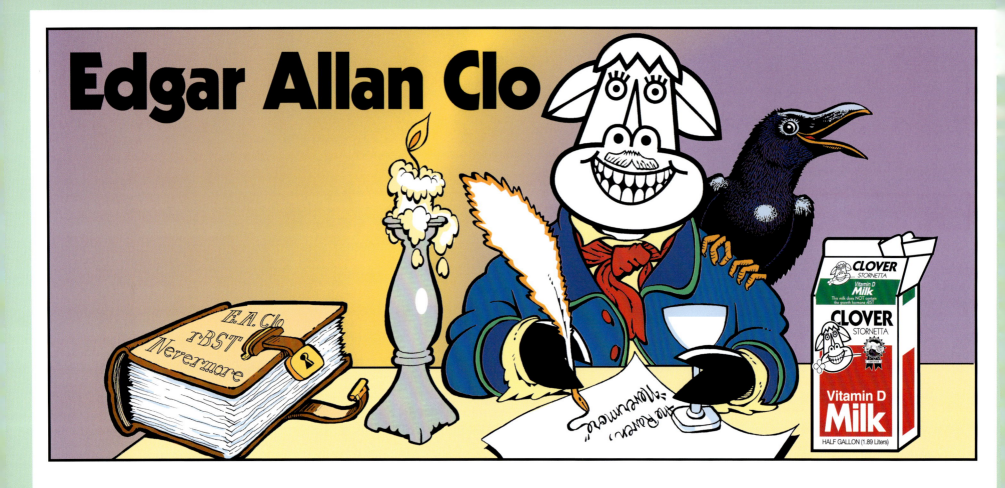

Clo-brainer:
How long are cows pregnant?

A: Nine months—just like people!

Fiddler on the Hoof

*Cottage Cheese production
Circa 1933*

1998

Blast from the Past:

Clover on the family table circa 1950's.

1999

Clo-brainer:
How far can a cow smell?

A: Cows have a great sense of smell and can smell something up to six miles away!

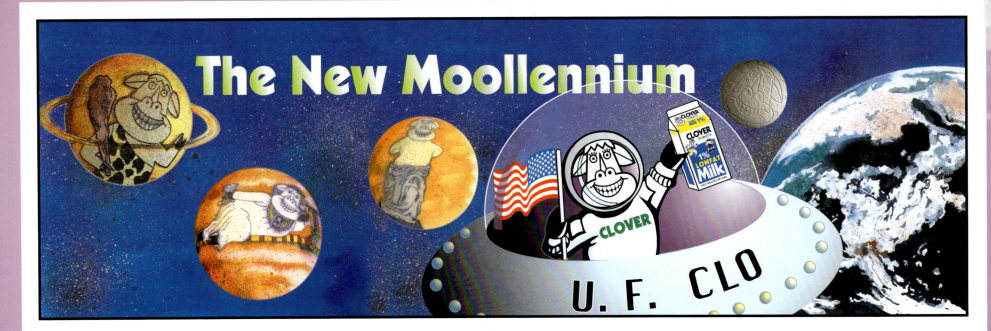

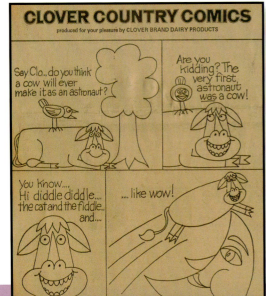

Q: Who was the first animal in space?

A: The cow that jumped over the moon.

1999

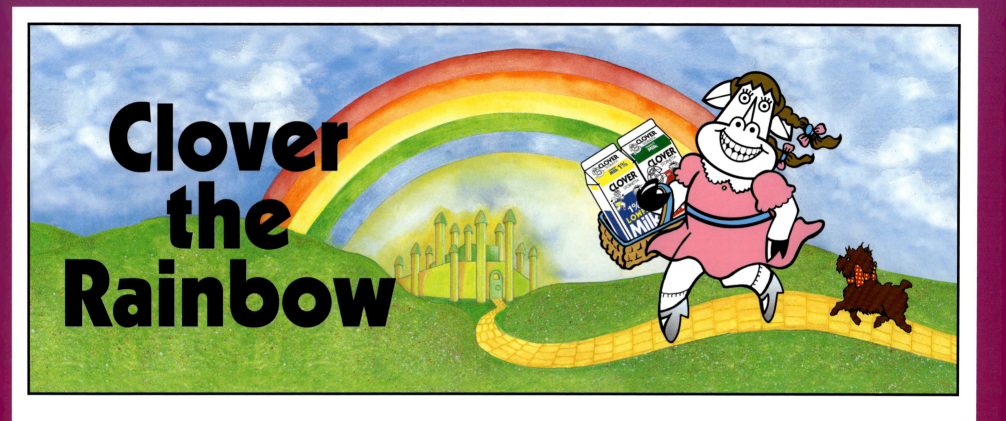

Q: *What's a cow's favorite moosical note?*

A: *Beef flat!*

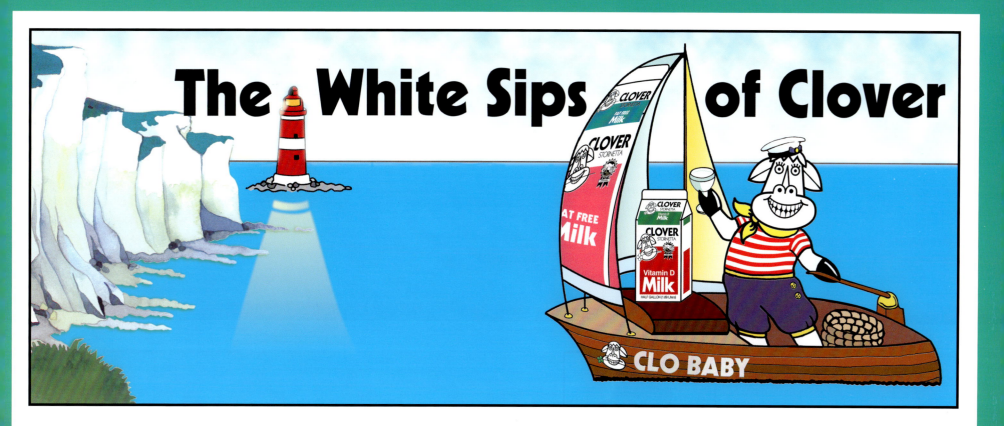

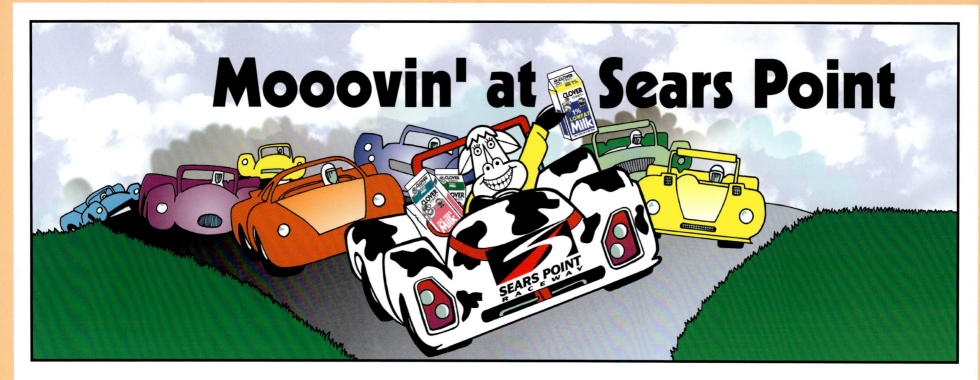

The need for speed...

Clover truck in front of Sanderson's, Petaluma circa 1930's.

2000

Udderly Striking

Cows like to sleep close to their families and sleeping arrangements are determined by an individual's rank in the hierarchy.

2000

Know the moo, feel the moo, be the moo.

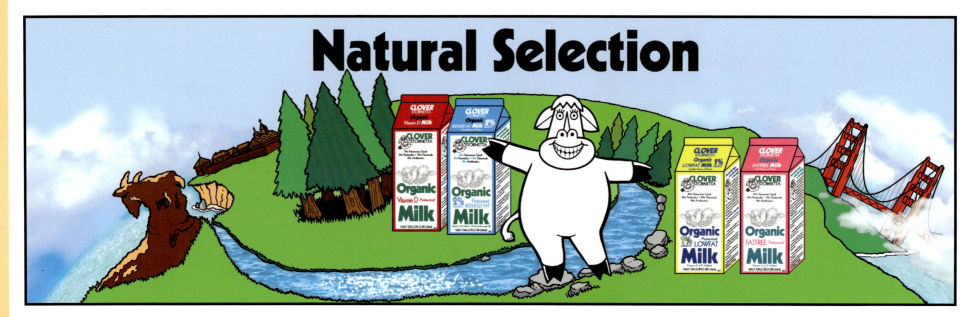

2001

Clo-brainer:

Can cows see color?

A: *Yes, but they are color-blind to red and green.*

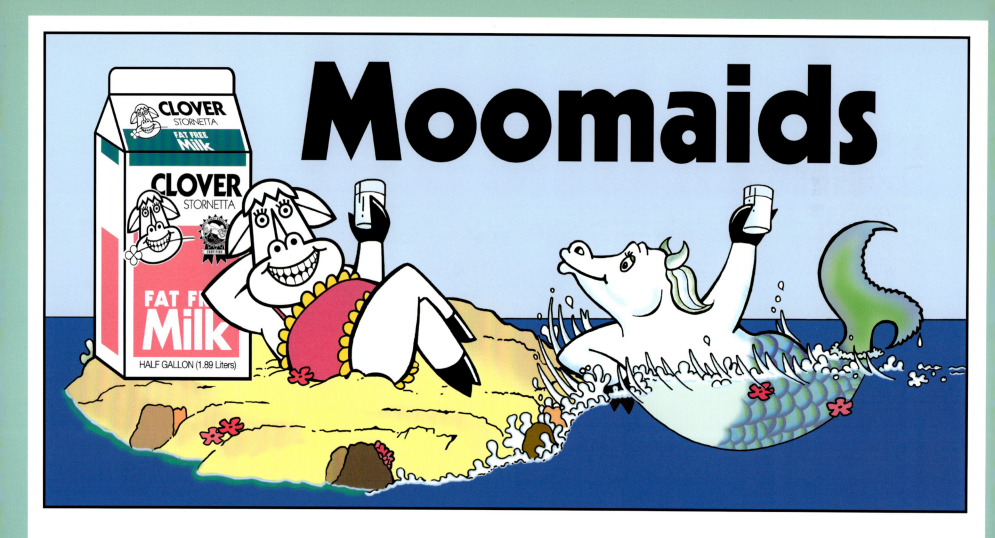

This was the first billboard that introduced the Clo babies, Lucky, Poppy, and Cookie.

2002

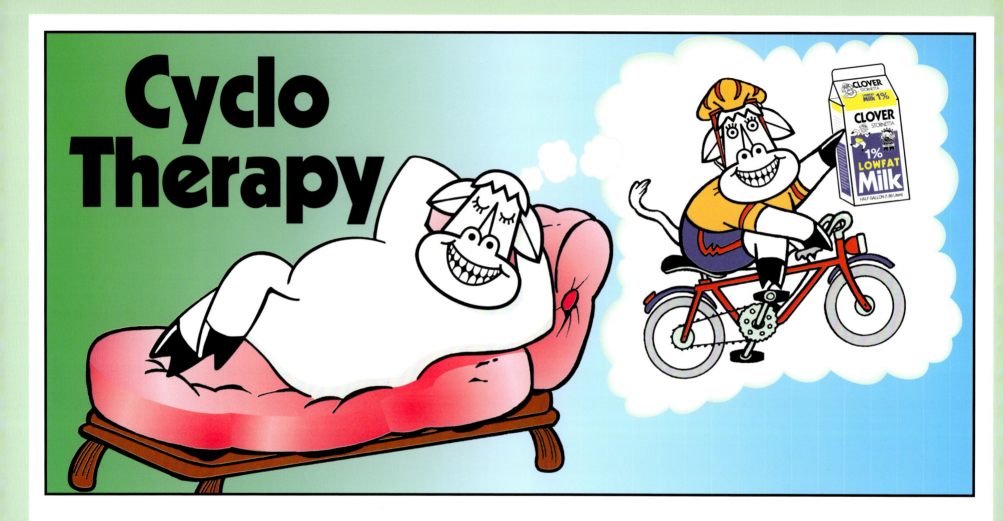

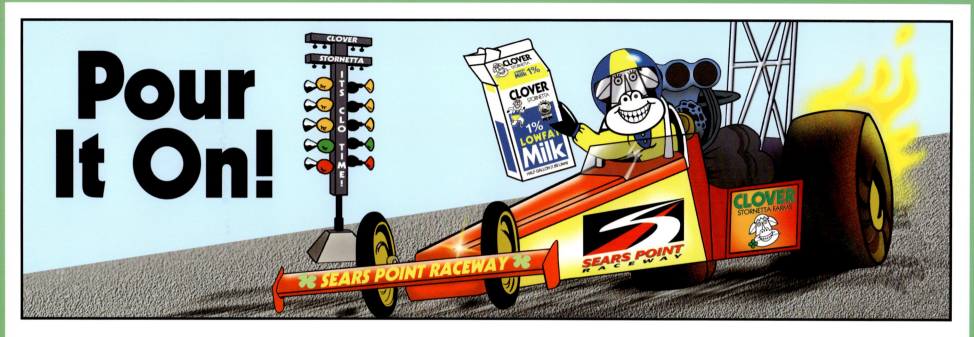

Clo and Clover have been through many generations of vehicles.

2002

Clo-brainer:

When were cows domesticated?

A: 5,000 years ago.

2002

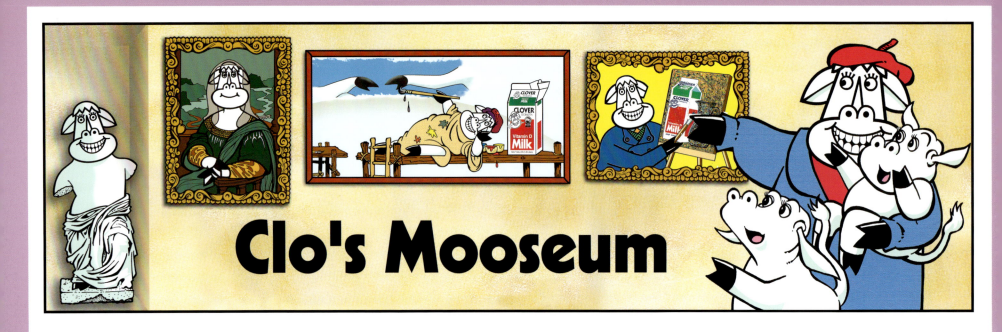

Clo-brainer:

How much feed does the average dairy cow consume each day?

A: 50 pounds.

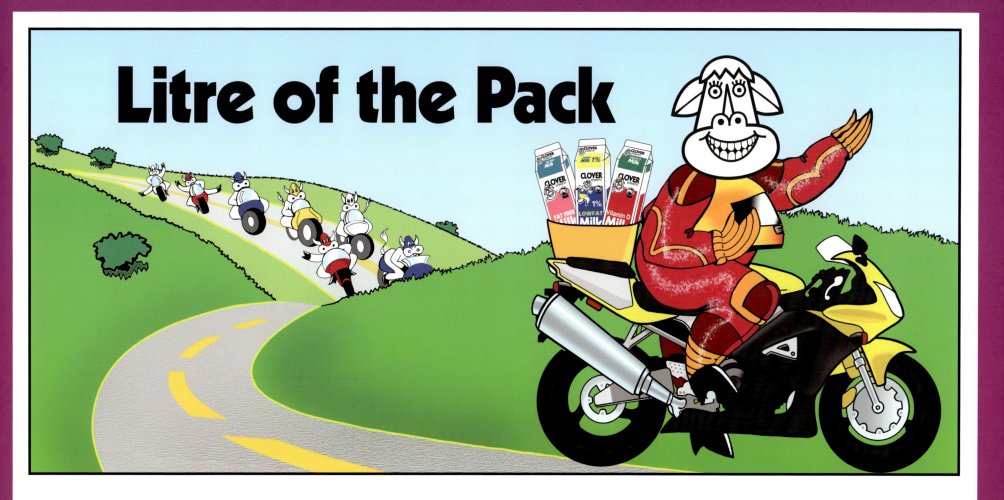

Q: What do you call a cow that plays a musical instrument?

A: A Mooo-sician.

Gene Benedetti with Al & Charlie Stornetta.

2003

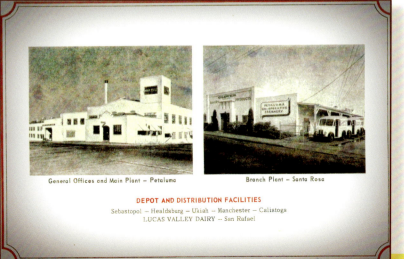

1963

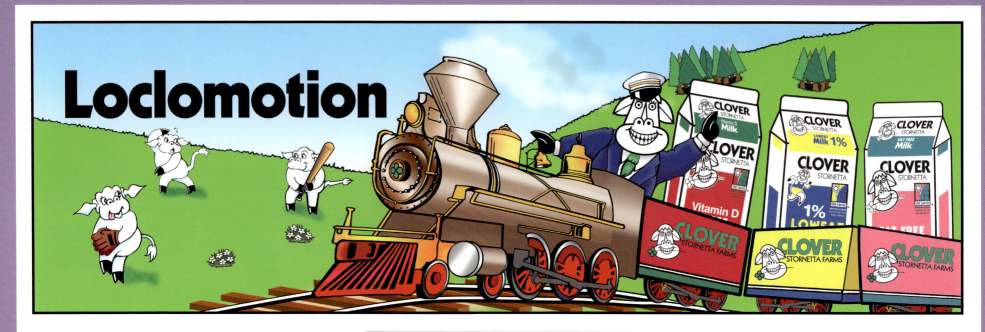

2004

This was the first appearance of Bullie Boy,
Clo's bedazzled admirer and ardent companion.

2004

Two ladies of Camoolot.

2004

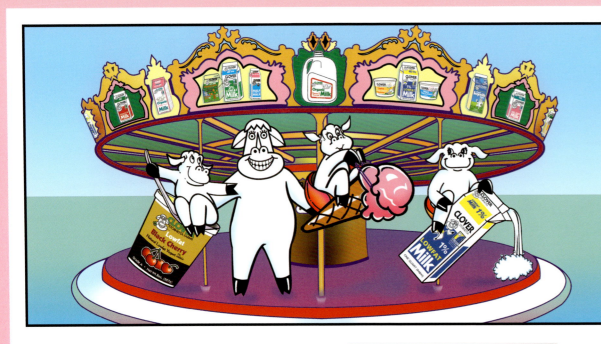

Merry Clo Round

What a ride!

2004

Clo-brainer:
Are horses and cows related?

A. Though both are hooved mammals and herbivores, horses are equids and cows are bovids, which are different species.

The Emporer's New Clo's

Check out the telephone numbers on this Vintage Clover Ad!

2005

Q: *Have you heard about the cow astronaut?*

A: *He landed on the moo-in!*

Cloleidoscope

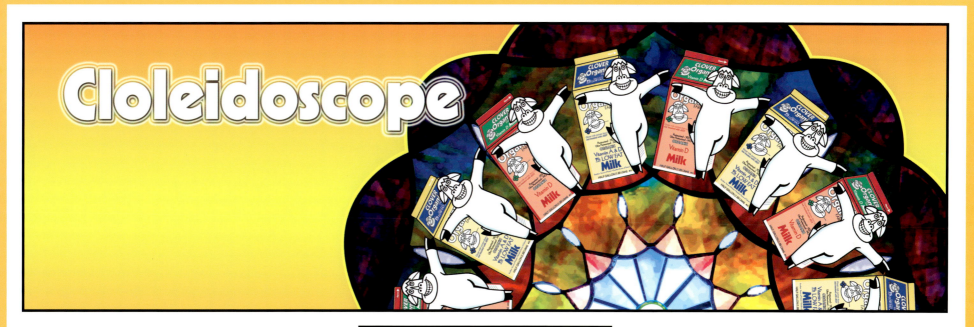

2006

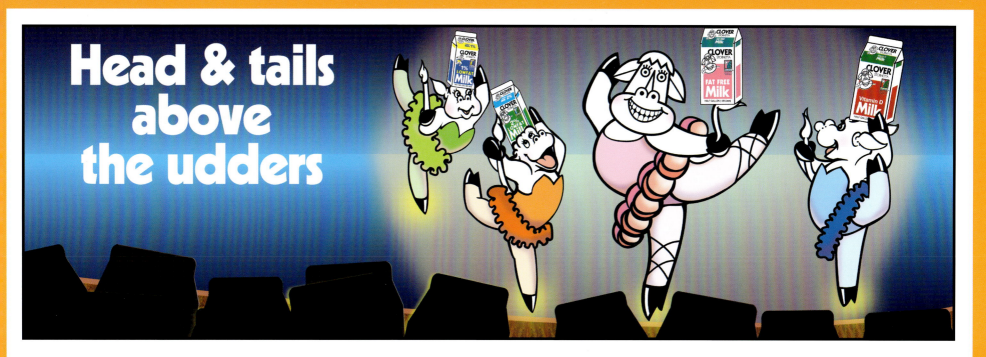

Directors – 1925

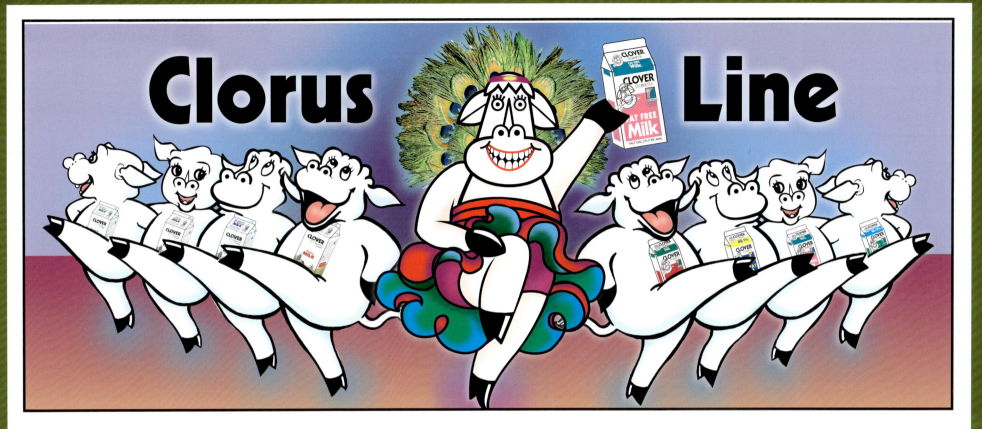

2006

Vintage Clover brand ad circa 1960's.

The heaviest live birth of a calf is 225 lbs for a British Friesian cow in 1961.

2007

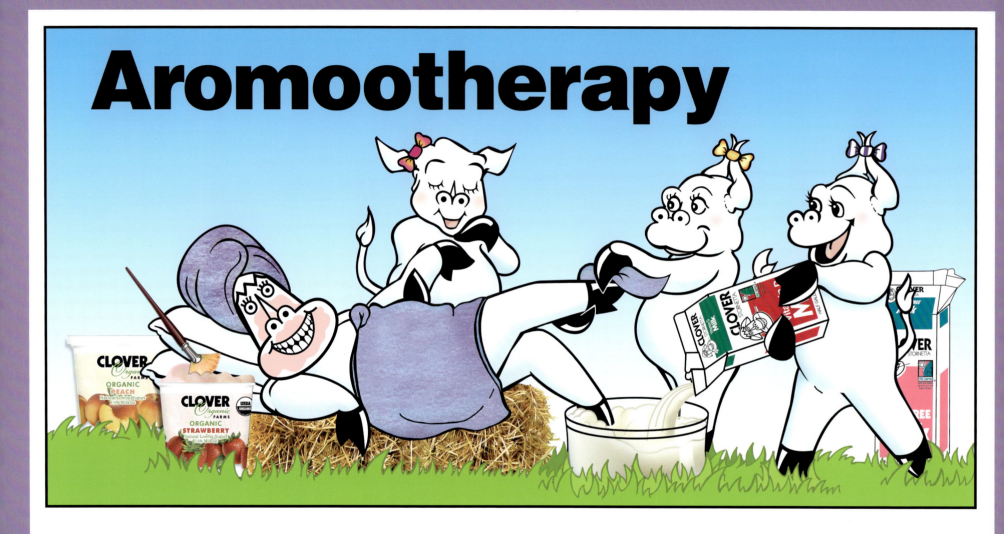

Cow Lick

Clo-brainer:

How many pints of ice cream does an average American consume in one year?

A: 48

2007

Clo-brainer:
How many bulls are in an average herd?

A: *There is 1 bull to every 30 cows.*

Clover Achiever

From left:

Herm Benedetti
Dan Benedetti
Bob St. Clair, Hall of Fame 49er
Gene Benedetti

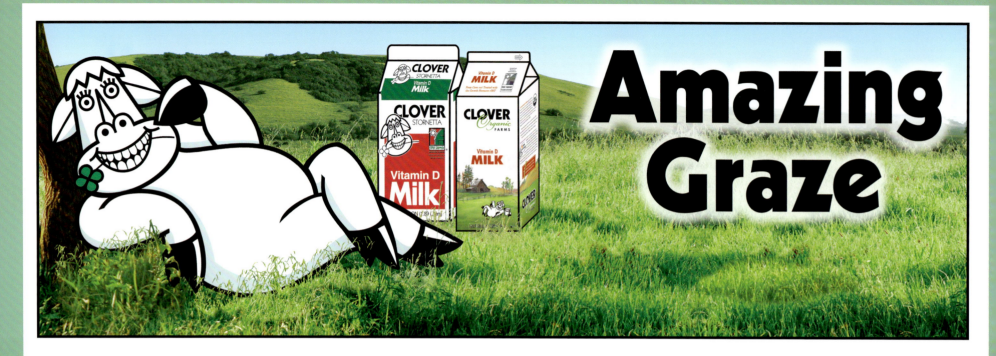

Yes, it is.

Cows spend 8 hours per day eating,
8 hours chewing her cud (regurgitated, partially digested food),
and 8 hours sleeping

Clover Girl

The Dairy Princess, another Clover Girl beauty!

2008

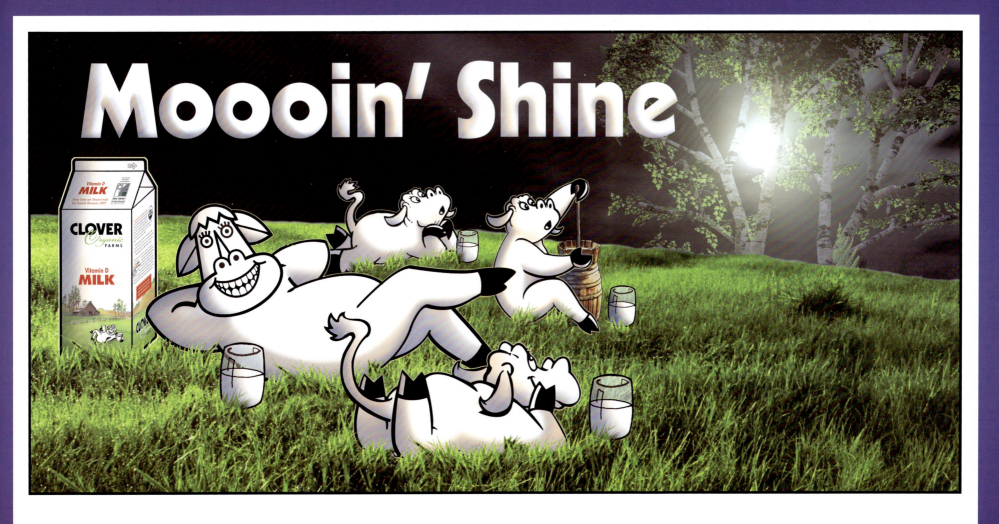

An udder day, an udder dollar.

2008

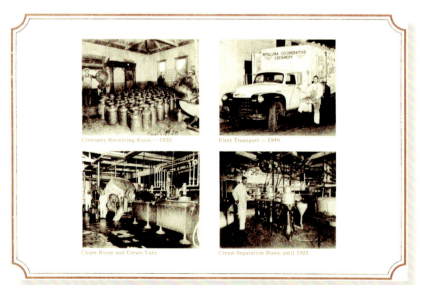

2008

Q: *Why does a milking stool have only 3 legs?*

A: *Because the cow has the udder.*

Q: What did the cow say to the silo?

A: Is my fodder in there?

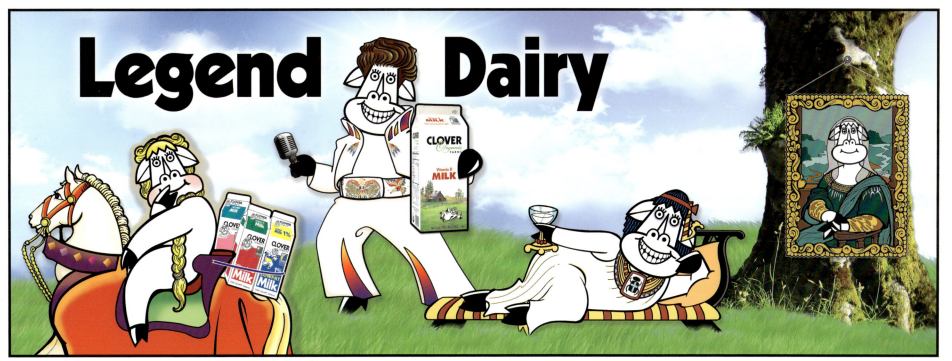

Other legendairy figures:

The Clo Washingtons

2009

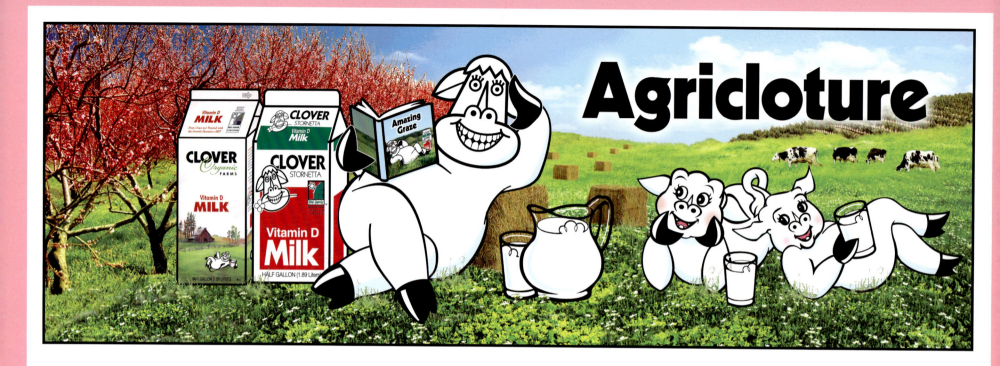

Sonoma County Fair Display:

Our milk is out of this world. Circa 1950's.

Q: What did the young bull sing to the cows in the other field?

A: "When I fall in love, it will be for heifer."

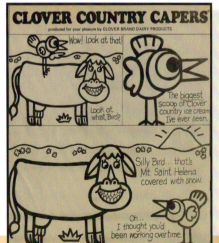

First Creamery — 1914

2009

The "Saclomento" version!

2009

2009 Billboard Contest Winner!

2010

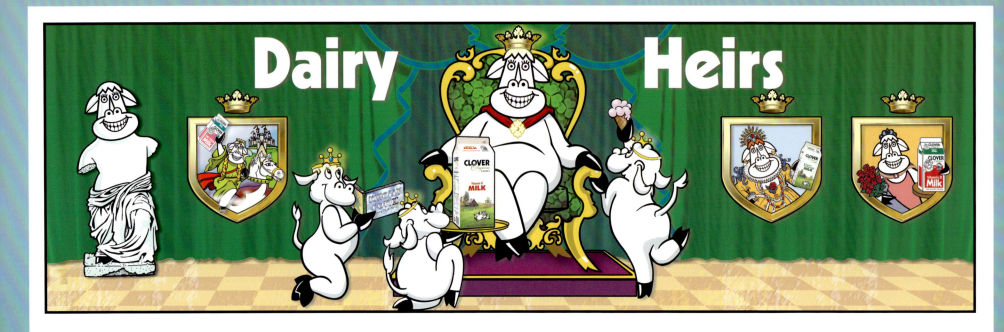

Q: What has four legs and goes Oom, Oom?

A: A cow walking backwards!

A remastering of the lovable 1969 billboard featured on page 38.

Queen of the Aisle

Q: How many times has Clo appeared as a Queen in this book? (This does not include Goddesses, Beauty or Fair contestant winners, Kings, Pharoahs, etc.)

A: 5

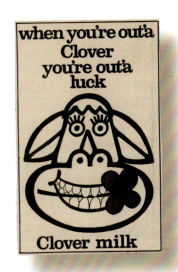

Q: *What does a cow Super-Villain say?*

A: *Moo-ha-ha-ha!*

Dairying young men on the flying trapeze

What a life:
Eat, graze, fly trapeze...

Directors and Management Group – Petaluma Co-operative Creamery 1963
(Director Paul Gambonini not shown)

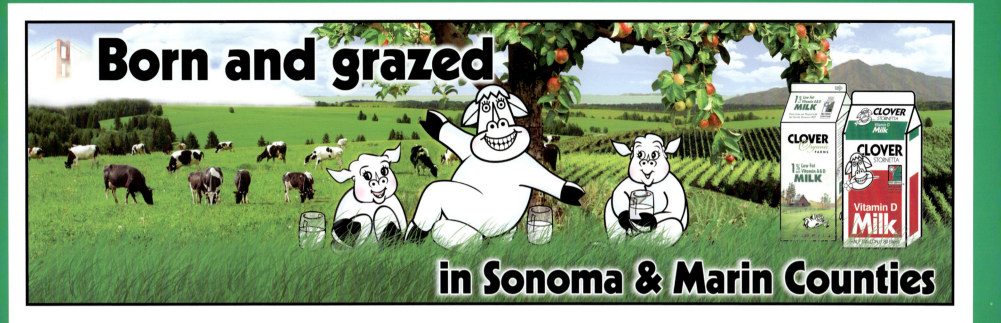

Clover's award-winning fleet, dedicated to providing fresh, healthy dairy products, & putting a smile on fellow road warrior's faces!

2012

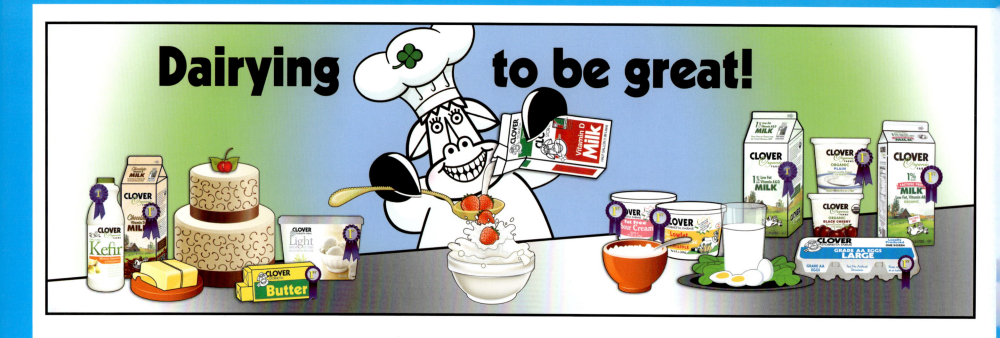

Clo & Guy Fieri "cheffing" it!

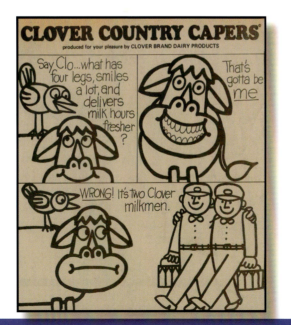

2012

Q: *What do cows do while skiing?*

A: *Moooo-Guts!*

2012

Like humans, cows form close friendships and choose to spend much of their time with 2-4 preferred individuals.

They also hold grudges for years and may dislike certain individuals.

Clo has a long history of cloture. She is shown here in a comfortable floral mooomooo as she contemplates her next sewing creation.

2012

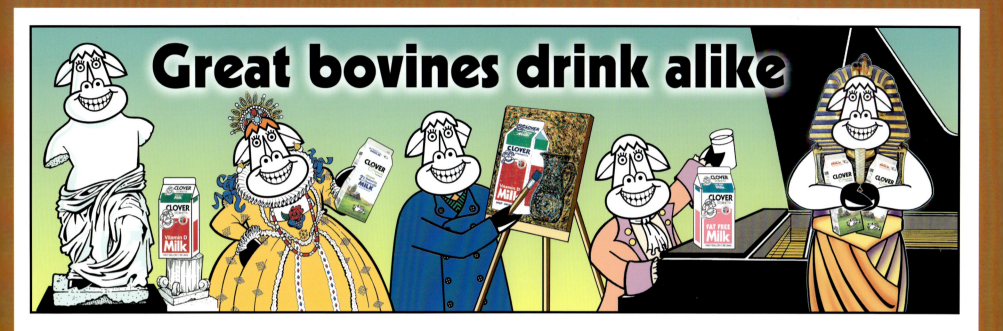

Q: *What do you call a sleeping bull?*

A: *A bull-dozer!*

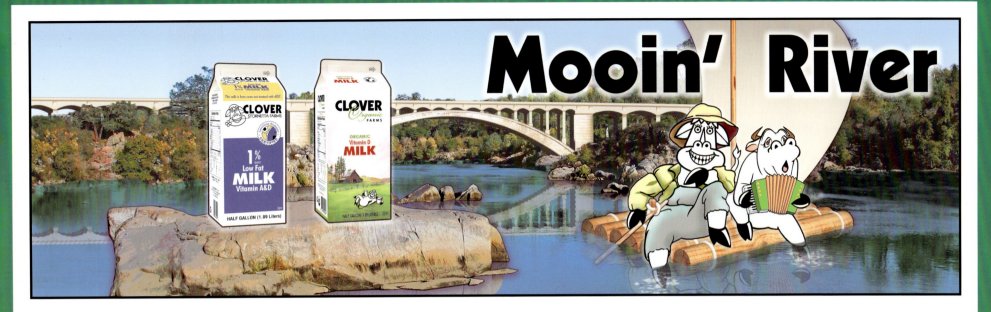

2013

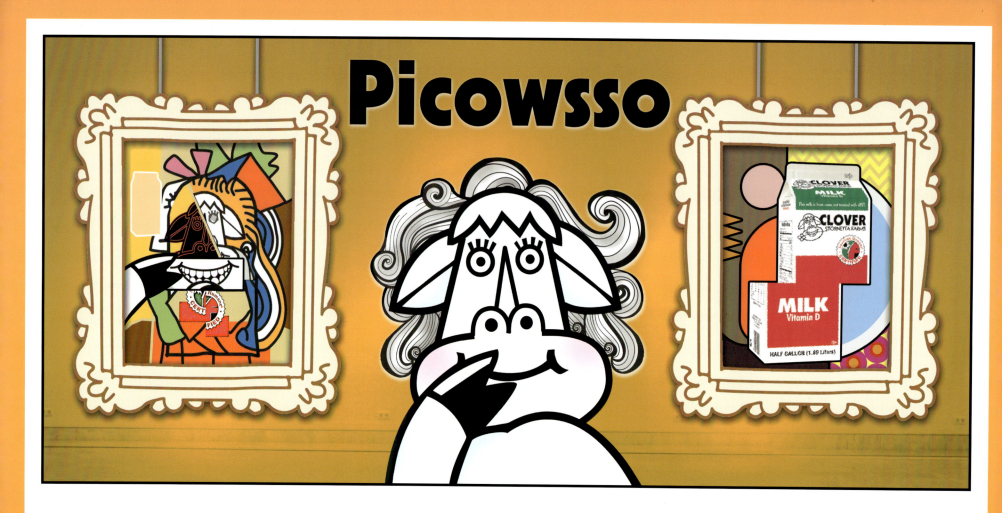

Clo-brainer:
How many jaw movements does a cow have on average every day?

A: 40,000

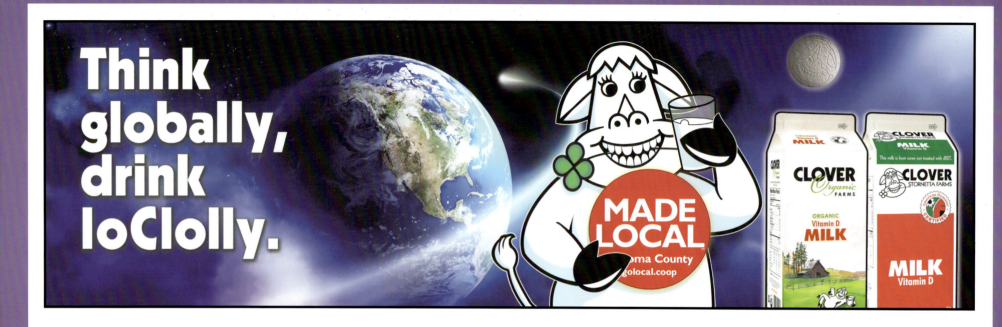

1970

2014
206

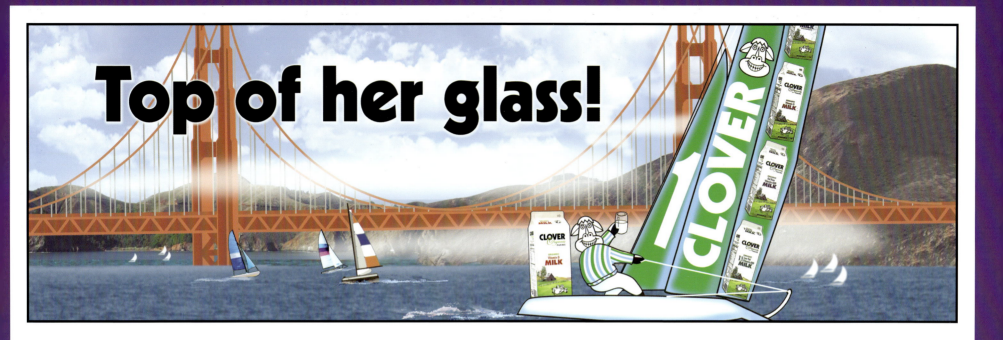

Clo-brainer:
You can lead a cow upstairs but not downstairs. Why?

A: A cow's knees can't bend properly to walk downstairs.

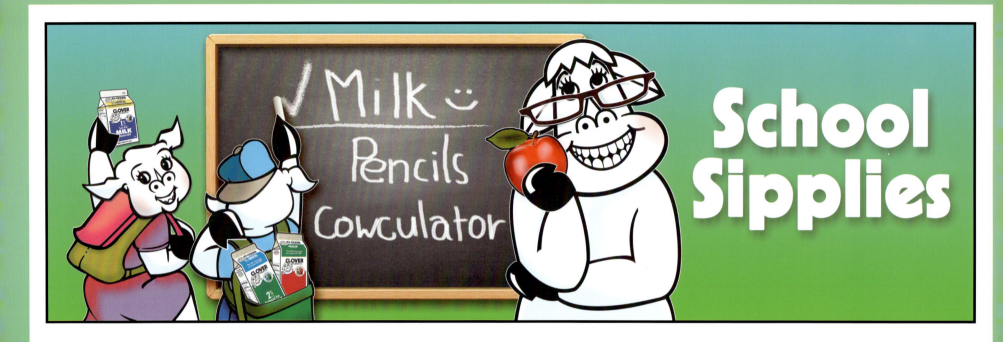

Q: What do you get when you cross an octopus and a cow?

A: An animal that can milk itself!

2014

Q: *What do you call an evil cow?*

A: *De-mooooon.*

The more you know, the more you Clo.

Q: *Why do cows have hooves instead of feet?*

A: *Because they lactose.*

Baby, It's Clo Outside!

Clo-brainer:
In what way is a Holstein dairy cow like a snowflake?

A: A Holstein's spots are like a fingerprint. No two cows have exactly the same pattern of black and white spots. They are all different.

Clo-brainer:
A single cow can produce enough milk in its lifetime to make _____ gallons of ice cream?

A: 9,000 gallons.

2015 radio campaign contest!

Straight Up Vanilla

Clo-brainer: *Which was invented first: Chocolate or Vanilla ice cream?*

A: Chocolate ice cream was invented long before vanilla, and the first documented recipe for it appeared in the book *The Modern Steward*, published in Italy in 1692.

Clo-brainer: *How much milk does it take to make one gallon of ice cream?*

A: 3 Gallons.

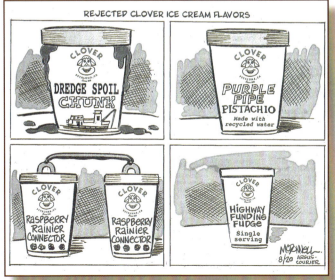

2015

Clo's preferred ride, Vintage cars.

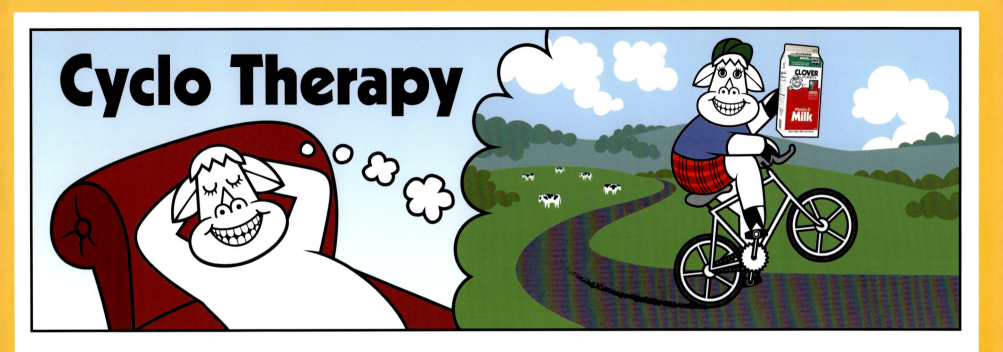

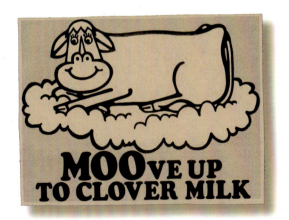

2015

Q: *What do you call our cow on Christmas?*

A: *Santa Clo!*

Vintage ad circa 1950's

Q: What do you call it when a cow gets loose?

A: Udder destruction!

In the life of creating a Clo billboard, many ideas are considered.

Here's one of our favorites that did not make the cut. Closeiden has to wait his turn!

2016

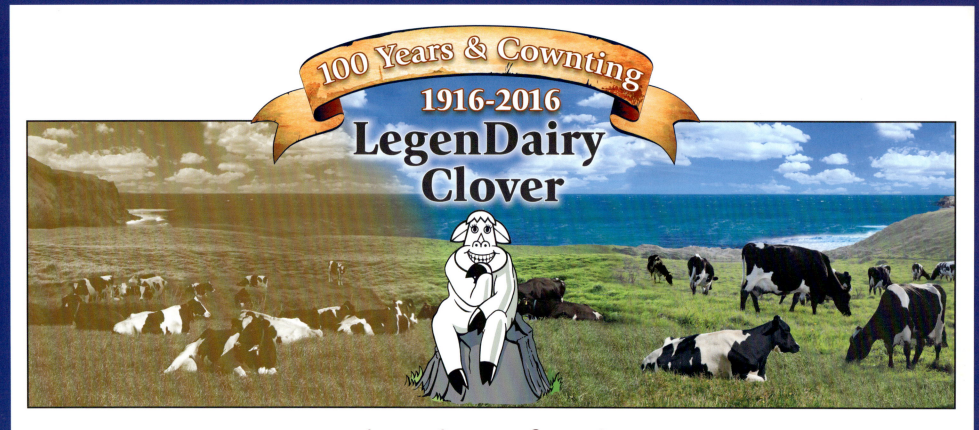

~ From the Clover family to you ~
Thank you for 100 years!